THE
DRAGON'S SECRET

AUGUSTA HUIELL SEAMAN

[ZHINGOORA BOOKS]

This edition is published by
Zhingoora Books.

CONTENTS

CHAPTER

CHAPTER I
THE NIGHT OF THE STORM

It had been a magnificent afternoon, so wonderful that Leslie hated to break the spell. Reluctantly she unrolled herself from the Indian blanket, from which she emerged like a butterfly from a cocoon, draped it over her arm, picked up the book she had not once opened, and turned for a last, lingering look at the ocean. A lavender haze lay lightly along the horizon. Nearer inshore the blue of sea and sky was intense. A line of breakers raced shoreward, their white manes streaming back in the wind. Best of all, Leslie loved the flawless green of their curve at the instant before they crashed on the beach.

"Oh, but the ocean's wonderful in October!" she murmured aloud. "I never had any idea *how* wonderful. I never saw it in this month before. Come, Rags!"

A black-and-white English sheep-dog, his name corresponding closely to his appearance, came racing up the beach at her call.

"Did you find it hard to tear yourself away from the hermit-crabs, Ragsie?" she laughed. "You must have gobbled down more than a hundred. It's high time you left off!"

She started to race along the deserted beach, the dog leaping ahead of her and yapping ecstatically. Twice she stopped to pick up some driftwood.

"We'll need it to get supper, Rags," she informed the dog. "Our stock is getting low."

He cocked one ear at her intelligently.

They came presently to a couple of summer bungalows set side by side about two hundred feet from the ocean edge. They were long and low, each with a wide veranda stretching across the front. There were no other houses near, the next bungalow beyond being about half a mile away.

With a sigh of relief, Leslie deposited the driftwood in one corner of the veranda of the nearest bungalow. Then she dropped into one of the willow rockers to rest, the dog panting at her feet. Presently the screen door opened and a lady stepped out.

"Oh! are you here, Leslie? I thought I heard a sound, and then it was so quiet that I came out to see what it meant. Every little noise seems to startle me this afternoon."

"I'm so sorry, Aunt Marcia! I should have called to you," said Leslie, starting up contritely to help her aunt to a seat. "I hope you had a good nap and feel rested, but sometimes I think it would do you more good if you'd come out with me and sit by the ocean than try to lie down in your room. It was simply glorious to-day."

Miss Marcia Crane shook her head. "I know what is best for me, Leslie dear. You don't always understand. But I believe this place *is* doing me a great deal of good. I confess, I thought Dr. Crawford insane when he suggested it, and I came here with the greatest reluctance. For a nervous invalid like myself to go and hide away in such a forsaken spot as this is in October, just you and I, seemed to me the wildest piece of folly. But I must say it appears to be working out all right, and I am certainly feeling better already."

"But why *shouldn't* it have been all right?" argued Leslie. "I was always sure it would be. The doctor said this beach was noted for its wonderfully restful effect, especially after the summer crowds had left it, and that it was far better than a sanatorium. And as for your being alone with me—why I'm sixteen and a quite competent housekeeper, as Mother says. And you don't need a trained nurse, so I can do most everything for you."

"But your school—" objected Miss Crane. "It was lovely of your mother to allow you to come with me, for I don't know another person who would have been so congenial or helpful. But I worry constantly over the time you are losing from high school."

"Well, don't you worry another bit!" laughed Leslie. "I told you that my chum Elsie is sending me down all our notes, and I study an hour or two every morning, and I'll probably go right on with my classes when I go back. Besides, it's the greatest lark in the world for me to be here at the ocean at this unusual time of the year. I never in all my life had an experience like it."

"And then, I didn't think at first that it could possibly be *safe*!" went on her aunt. "We seem quite unprotected here—we're miles from a railroad station, and not another inhabited house around. What would happen if—"

Again Leslie laughed. "We've a telephone in the bungalow and can call up the village doctor or the constable, in case of need. The doctor said there weren't any tramps or unwelcome characters about, and I've certainly never seen any in the two weeks we've been here. And, last but not least, there's always Rags!—You know how extremely unpleasant he'd make it for any one who tried to harm us. No, Aunt Marcia, you haven't a ghost of an excuse for not feeling perfectly safe. But now I'm going in to start supper. You stay here and enjoy the view."

But her aunt shivered and rose when Leslie did. "No, I prefer to sit by the open fire. I started it a while ago. And I'm glad you brought some more wood. It was getting low."

As they went in together, the girl glanced up at the faded and weather-beaten sign over the door. "Isn't it the most appropriate name for this place!—'Rest Haven.' It is surely a haven of rest to us. But I think I like the name of that closed cottage next door even better."

"What is it?" asked her aunt, idly. "I've never even had the curiosity to look."

"Then you must come and see for yourself!" laughed Leslie, turning her aunt about and gently forcing her across the veranda. They ploughed their way across a twenty-foot stretch of sand and stepped on the veranda of the cottage next door. It was a bungalow somewhat similar to their own, but plainly closed up for the winter. The windows had their board shutters adjusted, the door was padlocked, and a small heap of sand had drifted in on the veranda.

Leslie pointed to the sign-board over the door. "There it is,— 'Curlew's Nest.' There's something about the name that fascinates me. Don't you feel so too, Aunt Marcia? I can imagine all sorts of curious and wonderful things about a closed-up house called 'Curlew's Nest'! It just fairly bristles with possibilities!"

"What a romantic child you are, Leslie!" smiled her aunt. "When you are as old as I am, you'll find you won't be thinking of interesting possibilities in a perfectly ordinary shut-up summer bungalow. It's a pretty enough name, of course, but I must confess it doesn't suggest a single thing to me except that I'm cold and want to get back to the fire. Come along, dearie!"

Leslie sighed and turned back, without another word, to lead her aunt to their own abode. One phase of their stay she had been very, very careful to conceal from Miss Marcia. She loved this aunt devotedly, all the more perhaps because she was ill and weak and nervous and very dependent on her niece's care; but down in the depths of her soul, Leslie had to confess to herself that she was lonely, horribly lonely for the companionship of her parents and sisters and school chums. The loneliness did not always bother her, but it came over her at times like an overwhelming wave, usually when Miss Marcia failed to respond to some whim or project or bubbling enthusiasm. Between them gaped the abyss of forty years difference in age, and more than a score of times Leslie had yearned for some one of her own years to share the joy she felt in her unusual surroundings.

As they stepped on their own veranda, Leslie glanced out to sea with a start of surprise. "Why, look how it's clouding up!" she exclaimed. "It was as clear as a bell a few minutes ago, and now the blue sky is disappearing rapidly."

"I knew to-day was a weather-breeder," averred Miss Marcia. "I felt in my bones that a storm was coming. We'll probably get it to-night. I do hope the roof won't leak. We haven't had a real bad storm since we came, and I dread the experience."

At eight o'clock that evening it became apparent that they were in for a wild night. The wind had whipped around to the northeast and was blowing a gale. There was a persistent crash of breakers on the beach. To open a door or window was to admit a small cyclone of wind and sand and rain. Miss Marcia sat for a while over the open fire, bemoaning the fact that the roof *did* leak in spots, though fortunately not over the beds. She was depressed and nervous, and finally declared she would go to bed.

But Leslie, far from being nervous, was wildly excited and exhilarated by the conflict of the elements. When her aunt had finally retired, she hurried on a big mackinaw and cap and slipped out to the veranda to enjoy it better. Rags, whimpering, followed her. There was not much to see, for the night was pitch black, but she enjoyed the feel of the wind and rain in her face and the little occasional dashes of sand. Wet through at last, but happy, she crept noiselessly indoors and went to her own room on the opposite side of the big living-room from her aunt's.

"I'm glad Aunt Marcia is on the other side," she thought. "It's quieter there on the south and west. I get the full force of things here. It would only worry her, but I like it. How lonesome Curlew's Nest seems on a wild night like this!" She switched off her electric light, raised her shade, and looked over at the empty bungalow. Rags, who always slept in her room, jumped up on the window-seat beside her. The mingled sand and rain on the window prevented her from seeing anything clearly, so she slipped the sash quietly open, and, heedless for a moment of the drenching inrush, stood gazing out.

Only the wall of the house twenty feet away was visible, with two or three windows, all tightly shuttered—a deserted and lonely sight. She was just about to close her window when a curious thing happened. The dog beside her uttered a rumbling, half-suppressed growl and moved restlessly.

"What is it, Rags?" she whispered. "Do you see or hear anything? I'm sure there's no one around." The dog grumbled again, half audibly, and the hair along his spine lifted a little.

"Hush, Rags! For gracious sake don't let Aunt Marcia hear you, whatever happens! It would upset her terribly," breathed Leslie, distractedly. The dog obediently lay quiet, but he continued to tremble with some obscure excitement, and Leslie remained stock still, gazing at the empty house.

At length, neither seeing nor hearing anything unusual, she was about to close the window and turn away, when something caused her to lean out, regardless of the rain, and stare fixedly at a window in the opposite wall. Was she mistaken? Did her eyes deceive her? Was it possibly some freak of the darkness or the storm? It had been only for an instant, and it did not happen again. But in that instant she was almost certain that she had seen a faint streak of light from a crack at the side of one of the heavily shuttered windows!

CHAPTER II

FOUND ON THE BEACH

The next morning dawned windy and wet. A heavy northeast gale had whipped the sea into gray, mountainous waves. A fine drizzle beat in one's face through the slightest opening of door or window. Leslie loved the soft, salt tang of the air, and in spite of her aunt's rather horrified protests, prepared for a long excursion out of doors.

"Don't worry about me, Auntie dear!" she laughed gaily. "One can't possibly catch cold in this mild, beautiful air; and if I get wet, I can always get dry again before any damage is done. Besides, we need some more wood for the fires very, very badly and they say you can simply find heaps of it on the beach after a storm like this. I want some nice fat logs for our open fire, and I see at least a half dozen right down in front of this house. And last but not least, Rags needs some exercise!"

She found a wealth of driftwood at the water's edge that surpassed her wildest dreams. Again and again she filled her basket and hauled it up to the bungalow, and three times she carried up a large, water-soaked log balanced on her shoulder. But when the supply at last appeared ample, she returned to the beach on another quest. Rather to her surprise, she found that the stormy ocean had cast up many things beside driftwood—articles that in size and variety suggested that there must have been a wreck in the night.

Yet she knew that there had been no wreck, else the coast-guard station, less than a mile away, would have been very busy, and she herself must surely have heard some of the disturbance. No, there had been no wreck, yet all about her lay the wave-sodden flotsam and jetsam of many past disasters. A broken mast stump was imbedded upright in the sand at one spot. In another, a ladder-like pair of stairs, suggesting a ship's companionway, lay half out of the water. Sundry casks and barrels dotted the beach, some empty, some still untouched. Rusty tins of canned goods, oil, and paint, often intact, intermingled with the debris. Bottles, either empty or full of every conceivable liquid, added to the list; and sprinkled through and around all the rest were broken dishes, shoe-brushes, combs, and other household and personal articles in surprising quantities.

Leslie roamed about among this varied collection, the salt spray in her face, the surging breakers sometimes unexpectedly curling around her rubber boots. There was a new and wonderful fascination to her in examining this ancient wreckage, speculating on the contents of unopened tins, and searching ever farther and farther along the shore for possible treasure-trove of even greater interest or value

"Why *shouldn't* I find a chest of jewels or a barrel full of golden coins or a pocketbook crammed with bills, Rags?" she demanded whimsically of the jubilant dog. "I'm sure something of that kind must go down with every ship, as well as all the rest of this stuff, and why shouldn't we be lucky enough to find it?"

But Rags was busy investigating the contents of some doubtful-looking tin, and had neither time nor inclination to respond, his own particular quests being quite in another line and far more interesting to him!

So Leslie continued on her own way, absorbed in her own investigations and thoughts. The affair of the previous night was still occupying a large place in her mind. Nothing further had occurred, though she had watched at her window for nearly an hour. Even Rags at length ceased to exhibit signs of uneasiness, and she had gone to bed at last, feelin that she must have been mistaken in imagining anything unusual.

The first thing she had done this morning after leaving the house was to walk around Curlew's Nest, examining it carefully for any sign of occupation. It was closed and shuttered, as tight as a drum, and she could discern no slightest sign of a human being having been near it for days. But still she could not rid her mind of the impression that there had been*something* last night out of the ordinary, or Rags would not have behaved as he did. He was not the kind of dog that unnecessarily excited himself about nothing. It was a little bit strange.

"Oh, dear! I beg your pardon! I'm awfully sorry!" exclaimed Leslie, reeling backward from the shock of collision with some one she had unseeingly bumped into as she plowed her way along, her head bent to the wind, her eyes only on the beach at her feet. The person with whom she had collided also recovered a lost balance and turned to looked at her.

Leslie beheld a figure slightly taller than herself, clothed in yellow "slickers" and long rubber boots, a "sou'wester" pulled closely over plump, rosy cheeks and big, inquiring blue eyes. For a moment she could not for the life of her tell whether the figure was man or woman, boy or girl. Then a sudden gust of wind tore the sou'wester aside and a long brown curl escaped and whipped into the blue eyes. It was a girl—very little older than Leslie herself.

"Don't mention it!" laughed the girl. "I didn't know there was another soul on the beach beside Father and Ted and myself."

And then, for the first time, Leslie noticed two other figures standing just beyond, each clad similarly to the girl, and each with fishing-rod in hand and a long line running out into the boiling surf. The girl too held a rod in her hand.

"You just spoiled the loveliest bite I've had this morning," the girl laughed again, "but I'll forgive you if you'll tell me who you are and how you come to be out here in this bad weather. It's quite unusual to see any one on the beach at this season."

"I'm Leslie Crane, and I'm staying at Rest Haven with my aunt, Miss Crane, who is not well and is trying to recuperate here, according to the doctor's orders," responded Leslie, feeling somewhat like an information bureau as she said it.

"Oh, so you're staying here, are you? How jolly! I've never met any one staying here at this season before. I'm Phyllis Kelvin and this is my father and my brother Ted. Father—Miss Leslie Crane! Ted—"

She made the introductions at the top of her voice as the wind and roar of the ocean almost drowned it, and each of the two figures responded politely, keeping one eye all the while on his line.

"We always come down here for three weeks in October, Father and Ted and I, for the fishing," Phyllis went on to explain. "Father adores fishing and always takes his vacation late down here, so that he can have the fishing in peace and at its best. And Ted and I come to keep him company and keep house for him, incidentally. That's our bungalow right back there,—'Fisherman's Luck.'"

"Oh, I'm so glad you're going to be here!" sighed Leslie, happily. "I've been horribly lonesome! Aunt Marcia does not go out very often and sleeps a great deal, and I absolutely*long* to talk to some one at times. I don't know anything much about fishing, but I hope you'll let me be with you some, if I promise not to talk too much and spoil things!"

"You're not a bit happier to find some one than *I* am!" echoed Phyllis. "I love fishing, too, but I'm not so crazy about it as they are, and I've often longed for some girl chum down here. We're going to be the best of friends, I know, and I'll call on you and your aunt this very afternoon, if you'll come up to our bungalow now with me and help carry this basket of driftwood. Daddy and Ted won't move from the beach for the rest of the morning, but I'd like to stop and talk with you. I get tired sooner than they do."

Leslie agreed joyfully, and together they tugged a heavy basket of wood up to the one other bungalow on the beach beside the one Leslie and her aunt were stopping at—

and Curlew's Nest. She found Fisherman's Luck a delightful abode, full of the pleasant, intimate touches that could only be imparted by owners who inhabited it themselves most of the time. A roaring fire blazed invitingly in the big open fireplace in the living-room.

"Come, take off your things and stay awhile!" urged Phyllis, and Leslie removed her mackinaw and cap. The two girls sank down in big easy chairs before the fire and laughingly agreeing to drop formality, proceeded as "Phyllis" and "Leslie," to exchange confidences in true girl fashion.

"I mustn't stay long," remarked Leslie. "Aunt Marcia will be missing me and I must go back to see about lunch. But what a delightful bungalow you have! Are you here much of the time?"

"We're here a good deal in the off seasons—April to June, and September through November. Father, Ted, and I,—but we don't care for it so much in the summer season when the beach is more crowded with vacation folks and that big hotel farther up the beach is full. We have some cousins who usually take the bungalow for July and August."

"I never was at the ocean in October before," sighed Leslie, comfortably, "and it's perfectly heavenly! We have that dear little bungalow, Rest Haven, but the one right next to it is not occupied."

"No," said Phyllis, "and it's queer, too. I never knew either of them to be occupied at this season before. They are both owned by the Danforths, and they usually shut them both up on September and refuse to open them till the beginning of the next season. How did you come to get one of them, may I ask?"

"Oh, I think Aunt Marcia's doctor managed it. He happened to know the Danforths personally, and got them to break their rule, as a great favor to him. We appreciate it very much. But do you know," and here Leslie unconsciously sank her voice, "I saw such a queer thing about that other bungalow late yesterday evening!" And she recounted to her new friend a history of the previous night's experience.

"Oh, how perfectly gorgeous!" sighed Phyllis, thrilled beyond description by the narrative. "Do you suppose it's *haunted*? I've heard of haunted houses, but never of a haunted*bungalow!* Now don't laugh at me,—that's what Ted and Father do when I speak of such things," for Leslie could not repress a giggle at this suggestion.

"Phyllis, you *know* there are no such things as haunted houses—really!" she remonstrated.

"Well, I'm not so sure of it, and anyway, I've always *longed* to come across one! And what other explanation can there be for this thing, anyway? But do me one favor, won't you, Leslie? Let's keep this thing to ourselves and do a little investigating on our own account. If I tell Father and Ted and let them know what I think, they'll simply hoot at me and go and spoil it all by breaking the place open and tramping around it themselves and scaring away any possible ghost there might be. Let's just see if we can make anything out of it ourselves, will you?"

"Why of course I will," agreed Leslie heartily. "I wouldn't dare to let Aunt Marcia know there was anything queer about the place. She'd be scared to death and it would upset all the doctor's plans for her. I don't believe in the ghost theory, but I *do* think there may have been something mysterious about it, and it will be no end of a lark to track it down if we can. But I must be going now."

"I'm coming with you!" announced the impetuous Phyllis. "I want to go up there right away and do a little looking about myself. I simply can't wait."

So they set off together, trudging through the sand at the edge of the ocean, where the walking was easiest. All the way, Leslie was wondering what had become of Rags. It was not often that he deserted her even for five minutes, but she had not seen him since her encounter with Phyllis. It was not till their arrival at Curlew's Nest that she discovered his whereabouts.

Directly in front of this bungalow's veranda, and about fifty feet away from it, lay the remains of a huge old tree-trunk, half buried in the sand. Almost under this trunk, only his rear quarters visible, was the form of Rags, digging frantically at a great hole in the wet sand. So deep now was the hole that the dog was more than half buried.

"There's Rags! He's after another hermit-crab!" cried Leslie. "I was wondering where he could be." They both raced up to him and reached him just as he had apparently attained the end of his quest and backed out of the hole.

"Why, what has he got?" exclaimed Phyllis. "That's no hermit-crab!"

And in truth it was not. For out of the hole the dog was dragging a small burlap sack which plainly contained some heavy article in its folds!

CHAPTER III
THE MYSTERIOUS CASKET

Both girls dashed forward to snatch the dog's treasure-trove from him. But Rags had apparently made up his mind that, after his arduous labors, he was going to have the privilege of examining his find himself. At any rate, he would not be easily robbed. Seizing the burlap bag in his mouth, he raced to the water's edge and stood there, guarding his treasure with mock fierceness. Phyllis, being a stranger, he would not even allow to approach him, but growled ominously if she came within ten feet of his vicinity. And when Rags growled, it behooved the stranger to have a care! Leslie he pretended to welcome, but no sooner had she approached near enough to lay her hand on the bag than he seized it triumphantly and raced up the beach.

"Oh, do grab him, somehow!" cried Phyllis, in despair. "He'll drop the thing in the water and the next breaker will wash it away, and we'll never know what it was!"

Leslie herself was no less anxious to filch his treasure, but Rags had by now acquired a decidedly frolicsome spirit, and the chase he led them was long and weary. Three times he dropped the bag directly in the path of a breaker, and once it was actually washed out, and the girls groaned in chorus as they saw it flung into the boiling surf. But another wave washed it ashore, only to land it again in the custody of Rags before Leslie could seize it.

Finally, however, he wearied of the sport, and sensing the sad fact that his prize was in no wise edible, he dropped it suddenly to pursue an unsuspecting hermit-crab. The girls fell joyfully upon the long-sought treasure and bore it to the veranda of Curlew's Nest for further examination.

"What under the sun can it be?" marveled the curious Phyllis. "Something heavy, and all sewed up in a coarse bag like that! It's as good as a ghost story. Let's get at it right away."

They sat down on the wet steps while Leslie unrolled the bag,—not much larger than a big salt-bag,—and tried to tear an opening at the top. But her slender fingers were not equal to the task, so Phyllis undertook it.

"Let me try!" she urged. "I play the piano a great deal and my fingers are very strong."

And sure enough, it did not take her more than a moment to make an opening and thrust her hand into it. What she found there she drew out and laid in Leslie's lap, while the two girls gasped simultaneously at the singular object they had discovered.

To begin with, it was encrusted with sand and corroded by the contact of salt air and seawater. But when they had brushed off the sand and polished it as well as they could with the burlap bag, it stood forth in something of its original appearance—a small box or casket of some heavy metal, either bronze or copper, completely covered with elaborate carving. It was about six inches long, three wide, and two in height. It stood on four legs, and, upon examination, the carving proved to be the body of a winged serpent of some kind, completely encircling the box, the head projecting over the front edge where the lock or fastening of the cover would be. The legs of the receptacle were the creature's claws. The carving was remarkably fine and delicate in workmanship.

"My gracious!" breathed Phyllis. "Did you ever see anything so strange! What can it be?"

"And isn't it beautiful!" added Leslie. "What can that queer creature be that's carved on it? Looks to me like the pictures of dragons that we used to have in fairy-story books."

"That's just what it is! You've hit it! I couldn't think what it was at first—it's so wound around the box!" cried Phyllis. "But this thing is certainly a box of some kind, and there must be some opening to it and probably something in it. Let's try now to get it open."

But that was easier said than done. Try as they would, they could find no way of opening the casket. The dragon's head came down over the lock or clasp, and there was no vestige of keyhole or catch or spring. And so intricate was the carving, that there was not even any crack or crevice where the lid fitted down over the body of the box into which they could insert Phyllis's penknife blade to pry it open by force. The casket and its contents was a baffling mystery, and the wicked looking little dragon seemed to guard the secret with positive glee, so malicious was its expression!

Phyllis at last threw down her knife in disgust and rattled the box impatiently. "Something bumps around in there!" she declared. "I can hear it distinctly, but I don't believe we'll ever be able to get at it. I never saw such a queer affair! Let's try to break it with an ax. Have you one?"

"Oh, don't do *that!*" cried Leslie, horrified. "It would surely spoil this beautiful box and might even injure what's in it. There must be *some* other way of getting it open if only we take our time and go at it carefully."

They both sat for several moments regarding their find with resentful curiosity. Suddenly Leslie's thoughts took a new tack, "How in the world did it ever come there—buried in the sand like that?"

"Thrown up on the beach by the waves, of course," declared Phyllis, positively; "no doubt from some wreck, and buried in the sand after a while, just naturally, as lots of things are."

The explanation was a very probable one. "But it's rather far from the water's edge," objected Leslie.

"Oh, no, indeed! Why in winter the surf often comes up right under the bungalows!" remarked Phyllis, in quite an offhanded way.

"Mercy! Don't ever tell Aunt Marcia that, or she'd go straight home!" exclaimed Leslie. "But isn't it queer that it just happened to be right in front of Curlew's Nest! Everything queer seems to happen right around that place."

"That's so! I'd almost forgotten the other thing. But what *I* can't understand is how your dog happened to dig the thing up."

"Oh, that's simple! He's always chasing hermit-crabs—it's a great sport of his. And I suppose it just happened that one dug itself down in the sand right here, and he dug after it and then came across this."

Phyllis had a sudden brilliant idea. "Let's go and examine the hole! Perhaps there's something else in it."

They both raced over to the stump and Leslie thrust her hand into the hole. "There's nothing else in there," she averred, "but perhaps it might be worth while to dig around here and see if there might be some other article buried near it. I'll get a shovel."

She disappeared behind her own bungalow for a moment and returned with a shovel. They dug furiously for ten minutes and turned up the sand all about the original hole. Nothing of the slightest interest came to light, however, and they presently abandoned the attempt and filled in the hole again.

"This is all there was—that's plain," declared Phyllis, "and all we can think is that it was cast up from some wreck and got buried here."

But Leslie had been thinking. "Has it occurred to you, Phyllis, that it *might* have something to do with Curlew's Nest and the queer thing that happened here? I wonder how long it has been lying in that hole?"

They examined the find again. "I can tell you one thing," said Phyllis, "if it had been in that sand a *long* time, I think it would look rather different. To begin with, the burlap bag is in very good condition, whole and strong. It wouldn't take *very* long in there for it to become ragged and go to pieces. And besides that, the box would look different. You know that metal like this gets badly corroded and tarnished in a very little while when it's exposed even to this salt air, not to speak of the water too. I know, because we have some copper trays at the bungalow and they're always a *sight*! I have to keep polishing and polishing them to make them look nice. Now this box is very little tarnished since we rubbed it up. It makes me sure it hasn't been buried long."

"Well, has there been a wreck, then, very lately?" demanded Leslie.

"Not since last July—and that was only a fishing schooner. No chance in the world that such as *this* would be aboard of her!"

"Then, as far as I can see, this box must have been buried here—deliberately—and very recently, too!" declared Leslie, solemnly. "Can you think of any other explanation?"

"Leslie, could it have been done last night?" demanded Phyllis, in an awed whisper.

"Oh—I never thought of that. Perhaps it was. Perhaps that was the meaning of the light and all. Phyllis, there's some queer mystery here! I wonder if we ought to tell folks about it?"

"Oh *don't!*" implored Phyllis. "Not for a while, at least. It would be so wonderful to have this as a secret of our own and see what we can make of it. Just suppose we could work it out for ourselves!"

"Well—it *would* be a lark, and I only hope it's all right. But I'm going to ask you one favor, Phyllis. Please take the little box and keep it at your house, for I don't want Aunt Marcia to be worried about the matter, and she might come across it if I kept it here. And I must be going in now, or she'll be worried." And she thrust the box into Phyllis's hand.

"Indeed, I'll keep it gladly and hide it safely, too. This is one secret I won't have Ted meddling in!" declared Phyllis. "Let's call the box 'The Dragon's Secret.' He seems to be guarding very successfully! I'll come back this afternoon and call, and we can talk this over some more. Good-by!"

And she turned away toward the direction of her own bungalow, with "The Dragon's Secret" carefully concealed beneath her rainproof coat.

CHAPTER IV

IN THE SAND

The northeaster lasted three days. Then it blew itself out, the wind shifted to the northwest, and there was beautiful sparkling weather for the rest of the week.

During this time, the two new friends came to know each other very well indeed. It was not only their little shared mystery that united them—they found they had congenial tastes and interests in very many directions, although they were so different in temperament. Leslie was slight and dark in appearance, rather timid in disposition, and inclined to be shy and hesitant in manner. Phyllis was quite the opposite—large and plump and rosy, courageous and independent, jolly, and often headlong and thoughtless in action. Her mother had died when she was very little, and she had grown up mainly in the care of nurses and servants, from whom she had imbibed some very queer notions, as Leslie was not long in discovering. One of these was her firm belief in ghosts and haunted houses, which not even the robust and wholesome contempt of her father and older brother Ted had succeeded in changing.

But Phyllis had a special gift which drew the two girls together with a strong attraction: she was a devoted lover of music and so accomplished a pianist as to be almost a genius—for one of her age. The whole family seemed to be musical. Her father played the 'cello and Ted the violin, but Phyllis's work at the piano far surpassed theirs. And Leslie, too, loved music devotedly, though she neither sang nor played any instrument. It was a revelation to her when, on the next rainy afternoon, she accompanied Phyllis to the living-room of Fisherman's Luck and listened to a recital such as she had never expected to hear outside of a concert-hall.

"Oh, Phyllis, it's wonderful—simply wonderful!" she sighed blissfully when the last liquid ripples of a Chopin waltz had died away. "I don't see how you ever learned to play like that! But what in the world are you going to do now?" For Phyllis had jumped up with an impatient exclamation, laid back the cover of the grand piano, and was hunting frantically in the music cabinet for something.

"Why, I'm going to tune the old thing!" she declared. "This salt air is enough to wreck any piano, and this one is so old that it's below pitch most of the time. But of course it wouldn't do to have a very good one here. That's why Dad sent this one down. I just *had* to learn to tune it, in self-defense, or we could never have used it. So here goes!—" And, to Leslie's breathless amazement, she proceeded to tune the instrument with the most professional air in the world.

"Phyllis, you're amazing!" murmured Leslie, at length. "But, tell me—what do you intend to do with this wonderful gift you have? Surely you'll make it your career—or something like that!"

"Well, of course I *want* to," confided her friend. "To be candid—I'm crazy to. It's about the only thing I think of. But Father won't hear of it. He says he will let me have all the advantages he can, for an amateur, but that's all he's willing or can afford to do. Of course, I'm only seventeen and I've got to finish high school, at least. But I'm wild to go afterward to some one of the great European teachers and study for a year or two, and then see what happens. That, however, would cost at least two or three thousand dollars, and Father says he simply can't afford it. So there you are. It's awful to have an ambition and no way of encouraging it! But I'm always hoping that something will turn up." And Phyllis returned to her tuning.

"Two or three thousand dollars would be a pretty handy sum to have!" laughed Leslie. "I've been rather on the lookout for some such amount myself, but for a somewhat different reason."

"Oh, I'll warrant you have an ambition, too! Now tell me about it!" cried Phyllis, pouncing on her and ignoring the piano.

"Yes, it is an ambition," acknowledged Leslie, "but it isn't a bit like you. I hardly think you could call it an ambition—just a *wish*. You see, it's this way. We're rather a big family at home, four of us children, and I'm the oldest; and Father's rather delicate and has never been able to hold a good position long because he's out so much with illness. We get along fairly well—all but little Ralph. He's my special pet, four year old, but he's lame—had some hip trouble ever since he was a baby. He could be cured, the doctors say, by a very expensive operation and some special care. But we haven't the money for it—just yet. We're always hoping something will turn up, too, and my plan is to hurry through high school and training-school and then teach, and save every spare penny for Ralph. But it seems an awfully long time to wait, and all the while that little tot isn't getting any better."

There were tears in her eyes as she reached this point, and the impetuous Phyllis hugged her. "You darling thing! I think you're too unselfish for words! It makes me feel ashamed of my own selfish, foolish little wish. Wouldn't it be gorgeous if we could find four or five thousand dollars lying around on the beach? Wouldn't it just—" She stopped abruptly.

"What's the matter?" inquired Leslie. "Anything wrong?"

"No—something just occurred to me. What if that wretched little dragon of ours was guarding just such a fortune? It might be jewels or bank-notes or— or *something* equally valuable! I'm going to get it right away and make another try at opening it. It makes me furious, every time I think of it, to be so—so balked about getting at anything!"

"But, Phyllis," objected Leslie, "even if there *were* any such thing, I don't believe we'd have a right to keep it. It must belong to *somebody*, and we ought to make an effort to find out who. Don't you think so?"

"Oh, yes, if it's any *real* person—I suppose so," admitted Phyllis. "But what if—" She stopped significantly.

"Now *don't* tell me it was hidden there by *ghosts!*" And Leslie's infectious laugh pealed out.

"Oh, hush! or Ted will hear. He can't be far away," implored Phyllis, guiltily. "Of course, I don't say what or whom it was hidden by, but there's something mighty queer to me about an empty bungalow being inhabited by *living folks*—"

"What about burglars?" interrupted Leslie, quickly.

"Never *was* such a thing around these parts, in any one's experience!" Phyllis hastened to assure her, much to her secret relief.

"Then perhaps it's the people who own the cottage," offered Leslie.

"No chance. They've all gone off to spend the winter in California—every one. Ted had a letter from Leroy Danforth, who is a great chum of his, last week."

"Well, I *know* there is some other explanation besides a—a ghostly one!" declared Leslie, nothing daunted. "But anyway, we might have another look at the dragon."

Phyllis went and got it out from its hiding-place in her trunk, and they spent a fruitless half-hour wrestling with its secret fastening. They broke their finger-nails trying to pry it open, they pressed and poked every inch of it in an endeavor to find a possible secret spring; they rattled and shook it, rewarded in this case by the dull thud of something shifting about. It was this last sound only that kept up their courage. Finally they gave it up.

"I believe we could break it open with an ax, perhaps; but you don't seem to approve of that, so how we're ever going to find out, I'm sure I can't imagine!" declared Phyllis, discouraged.

"Do you know, I think this metal is so strong it would resist even an ax," Leslie soothed her, "and we'd only damage the box without accomplishing anything. There must be some other way. Why not show it to Ted and your father? Perhaps they could do what we can't."

"I will *not* share this secret with Ted!" declared Phyllis, obstinately. "He's nearly nineteen and he thinks he's the most important thing in creation, and he's perfectly insufferable in some ways, now. To have his advice asked in this thing would set him up worse than ever. I won't do it!"

Leslie had to smile inwardly at this outburst. To her, Ted had seemed just a jolly, agreeable, and rather companionable boy, with a very friendly, likable attitude. But she realized that she had not had Phyllis's sisterly experience, so she said nothing more. They put the dragon back in his hiding-place and sadly admitted themselves more baffled than ever.

On the evening of the third day after this, however, a strange thing happened.

To the surprise of Leslie, Miss Marcia had been induced to walk along the beach, after supper, and stop in at Fisherman's Luck to hear a concert—an impromptu one—given by Phyllis and her father and brother. Leslie had learned that the Kelvin family amused itself in this fashion every night when the fishing was not particularly good.

"I'd love to hear them play, shouldn't you, Aunt Marcia? Phyllis is a wonder, just by herself, and they must make a delightful trio!" She said this without any hope that her aunt would express much interest; but to her astonishment, Miss Marcia replied:

"Well, suppose we walk down there after tea. I'm feeling so much better that I don't believe it would hurt me, and I'm just hungry to hear some music myself!"

Leslie joyfully imparted the news to Phyllis, and they planned an elaborate program. It was an evening that they long remembered, so absorbed were they in the music that they all loved. And it was not till the end of an ensemble rendering of a Bach concerto, that some one remarked, "Why, it's raining!"

No one had noticed it until then. Miss Marcia was quite aghast, for she seldom ventured out in the rain and she had brought no adequate wraps. But Leslie settled that question speedily. "I'll take Rags and run up the beach to our bungalow and bring them to you, if Phyllis will lend me her slickers," she declared. "No, you mustn't come with me, Ted. I'll be perfectly safe with Rags, and while I'm gone, you can all be giving that Beethoven sonata that you promised Aunt Marcia. I won't be fifteen minutes."

They finally let her go and settled down to the music once more. She was much more than fifteen minutes in returning, but no one noticed it, so deeply immersed were they in the rendering of the sonata. At last, however, she was back, breathless and dripping and with a curious light in her eye that no one noticed but Phyllis.

"What is it?" Phyllis managed to whisper, when the others were talking and putting on wraps.

"Just this," replied Leslie, breathlessly and jerkily. "While I was in the house—I happened—to look out of my window—as I often do,—no light in my room—and I saw—that light again next door! Rags saw it too—at least he growled in that queer way. I waited and watched a long time—I wanted to go out nearer the place—but didn't dare. Then it disappeared and I didn't see it—any more. Then I came on here."

Phyllis listened to the whispered, jerky sentences in a thrilled silence. Then she replied: "I'm coming up first thing to-morrow morning—early! But watch out the rest of the night—if you can!"

Phyllis was as good as her word—better, in fact, for she was actually knocking at the door of Rest Haven before Leslie was out of bed, much to Miss Marcia's astonishment.

"Did you see anything else?" was her first whispered greeting.

But Leslie shook her head. "There wasn't another thing happened. I watched nearly all night—till I fell asleep at the window, in fact!"

"Well, something happened at *some* time or other!" replied Phyllis, provocatively.

"How do you know?" demanded Leslie, in a twitter.

"I've seen the sign of it. Come outside and I'll show you!"

They made some excuse to Miss Marcia for immediately vacating the house, and hurried outdoors. Phyllis led the way to a certain side door of Curlew's Nest, on the opposite side from Rest Haven, where a sheltering projection of roof extended out for two or three feet over the ground. The hard rain of the night before had beaten out the sand all about the wooden foot-path to an unbroken smoothness. But just under the protecting roof, Phyllis pointed to something at their feet.

"There it is!" she muttered. And Leslie, staring down, beheld the impression of a single footprint—a footprint very different from either of their own—in the sand!

CHAPTER V

AN EXPLORING PARTY

"Well!" was Leslie's first remark, "that proves *one* thing beyond a doubt."

"What?" demanded Phyllis.

"That it wasn't a *ghost* around here. I never yet heard of a ghost who made a footprint!"

The deduction somewhat staggered Phyllis in her pet belief. "I suppose that's true," she had to admit. "I never did, either. But now the question is, who did it and what did he want?"

But Leslie had been carefully examining the footprint. "You say, what did 'he' want. Have you noticed that this footprint doesn't look very much like a *man's*?"

Phyllis stooped over it. "You're right! It's a woman's or a girl's. Here's the deep imprint of the little French heel, and the narrow, pointed toe. Must have a mighty small foot!" She measured her own beside it. "Still, even mine would look much smaller in pumps or slippers instead of these comfortable sneakers. Might be either a small woman or a girl like ourselves."

"But why is there only *one*, I wonder?" mused Leslie.

"I think the answer to that is simple. She walked on this narrow board-walk up from the back road, probably because it was easier, or, even perhaps, so as not to make any footprints. And just at the doorstep she may have stumbled, or stepped off by mistake in the darkness. Perhaps she didn't even realize it."

Again Leslie had bent over the footprint. "She was coming in when she made it. Do you notice that it points toward the door?"

Phyllis stared at her. "What a perfectly dandy detective you'd make!" she exclaimed. "You simply take in everything!"

"You're just as good and even better!" laughed Leslie, secretly pleased, however.

"Hurrah for us!" cried Phyllis. "We're just a pair of natural *Sherlock Holmeses*! Now, here's what I propose. There's something mighty queer going on here, I believe. And

I'm willing to give up my ghost theory, because it *does* seem silly. But I want to investigate the thing pretty thoroughly, and the only way to do it is to get into that bungalow and see what has been going on inside."

"But Phyllis!" cried the shocked Leslie. "You wouldn't break into some one else's bungalow, would you? And besides, how *could* you?"

"Pooh!" declared Phyllis, in scorn. "As if I didn't know this bungalow as well as our own, and the Danforths almost as well as my own family, too, for that matter. I've been in here a thousand times. The Danforths would be only too grateful to me for keeping an eye on their place for them. They'd do the same for us. And as for getting in—why, I've always known a private way of getting in when everything's locked up. The Danforths themselves showed me. We'll get in this afternoon. This morning I promised Ted and Father I'd fish with them awhile; but this afternoon I'm free."

"Where are you two girls?" they heard Miss Crane calling from next door, and they started guiltily, not realizing how long they had been away.

"I must be more careful, or Aunt Marcia will begin to suspect something and question me," whispered Leslie. "It would never do in the world to have her realize there was anything queer going on so close to us. She'd pack up for home in a minute, her nerves are still so uncertain. Coming, Aunt Marcia!"

"That's so!" agreed Phyllis. "Between keeping it from your aunt and from Ted and Father, we're going to have some tight squeezes, I foresee! Well, I'll be back after luncheon and we'll do a bit of investigating. Good-by!"

It was between half past one and two, that afternoon, when Phyllis again appeared at Rest Haven—a very auspicious time, for Miss Marcia was in her room taking her usual long nap and Ted and his father had gone a mile or more down the beach to an inlet to try the fishing there. The two girls had the whole vicinity to themselves.

"What shall we do with Rags?" questioned Phyllis. "I hardly think we ought to take him in. Can't you chain him up?"

"Oh, I wouldn't dare! He'd howl himself sick and wake Aunt Marcia. You see, he's never chained. But I can turn him loose on the beach and let him chase hermit-crabs, and when he's well occupied, we can slip away."

They strolled down to the water's edge with the dog, who was speedily absorbed in the one occupation he found of never-failing interest. Then they slipped back to the bungalow without his even noticing that they had gone.

It was only when they stood by the side door of Curlew's Nest that Leslie noticed something bulky concealed under Phyllis's sweater.

"What in the world have you got there?" she demanded.

Phyllis produced a large-sized electric torch. "How do you suppose we are going to see anything in that dark place without something like this? We certainly mustn't open any windows."

Leslie confessed she hadn't thought of it, and then watched with amazement while Phyllis skilfully inserted the blade of a knife in the crack of the door, wiggled it about a moment, and triumphantly lifted the hook inside from its ring and swung open the door.

"Hurry in!" she whispered. "We must close this quickly before any one can notice."

They shut the door in haste, and Phyllis flashed on her light. Then she replaced the hook in its ring. "Now we're safe! You see, this is a little side-closet like a pantry, where the ice-box is kept. They had the door made so that the ice need not be carried in through the kitchen."

"But that's a very poor catch for the door—just that little hook!" cried Leslie. "I should think they'd have something more secure than that."

"I suppose it is," agreed Phyllis, "and they've often said so themselves. And yet it's just one of those things that never gets changed. Anyhow, nobody ever locks anything down here, only fastens things up when the season is over. There's really nothing valuable enough here to lock up or to be attractive to thieves. And so it has just gone on, and I suppose that hook will remain there forever! But come along! Let's get down to business. This way to the living-room!" and she led the way along a passage and into the big main room of the bungalow.

It was very much on the style of that of Rest Haven, furnished with attractive willow furniture, and with a large brick open fireplace at one side. As Phyllis flashed the torch about in a general survey, Leslie noticed that the cottage was obviously dismantled for the winter. The furniture stood huddled against the walls; there were no dainty draperies at the shuttered windows, and the rugs were rolled up, tied, and heaped in one corner.

"Nothing seems out of the way here," said Phyllis. "It's just as the Danforths usually leave it. Now let's look into the bedrooms."

They journeyed through the four bedrooms with no different result. Each wore the same undisturbed air of being shorn of its summer drapery, with beds starkly stripped of all but their mattresses, and these covered with heavy paper. Then on into the kitchen, which seemed, of all the rooms, to wear more nearly its normal aspect. But even there everything, apparently, appeared as it should.

It was in the kitchen that Phyllis stopped short and faced Leslie. "Well, doesn't it beat everything!" she exclaimed. "After all we've seen and heard,—yes, and *found*,— there's not a thing here that looks as if a living soul had been in it since Mrs. Danforth closed it up. Now what do you make of it?"

"Perhaps we haven't looked closely enough. Let's go over it again," was all Leslie could offer. "And isn't it possible that a person might come in here for some reason and not disturb anything?"

"Yes, of course it's possible, but is it likely?" countered Phyllis. "But as you say, we'd better go over the place again and more carefully. If we don't find *something*, I shall certainly go back to believing in my 'ghost.' And I guess you'll admit I have foundation for it now!"

Phyllis flashed the torch about in a general survey

"I tell you what!" suggested Leslie. "Suppose we each take a turn with the flash-light and go over every room twice, first you, then myself. I noticed that, when you held the light, I had to follow behind and look over your shoulder or get in your way, and I really couldn't see very well. Now, I'll sit in this chair while you go over the place, and then you give the torch to me. How does that strike you?"

"Good idea! You're full of 'em, Leslie. I ought to have thought of it before." And while Leslie sat down rather gingerly in one of the willow rockers against the wall, Phyllis systematically examined the room again, diving into all the nooks and corners, and at last came back to hand the torch to her friend.

"No luck! It's as clean as a whistle of any clues, as far as I can see. You take your turn."

When Leslie had completed her search, they proceeded to treat the other rooms in similar fashion, and so had come to the last bedroom when they were startled by a sound from outside the house.

"What in the world is *that*?" cried Phyllis, in a panic. "It's the most uncanny sound I ever heard!" They listened again and caught the intonation of a long moan, ending in a rising note like a wail. It was truly a little hair-raising in the closed, forsaken spot.

Suddenly Leslie giggled. "Oh, it's only Rags! He's missed me at last, traced me here, and is probably sitting by that side door now, protesting against having been deserted!"

Phyllis was both relieved at the explanation and annoyed at the interruption. "Let's go and stop him right away, or he'll have all the neighborhood here!"

They hurried to the little side door in the pantry and snapped off their light. Rags, from the outside, sniffing at the threshold, sensed their approach and yapped joyously.

"But how are you going to lock that door after you?" whispered Leslie, in sudden terror. "It isn't possible!"

"Trust me!" smiled the capable Phyllis. "Do you suppose I'd have unfastened it if I couldn't fasten it up again? I just keep the hook in a certain position with my knife, as I close the door, and then gently drop it into the ring through the crack. I've done it a dozen times. Leroy Danforth taught us how."

Leslie breathed a sigh of relief, and Phyllis cautiously opened the door.

Then both girls started back in genuine dismay!

Sitting cross-legged in the sand, directly in front of the door and holding back the delighted Rags by his collar, was—of all people most unwelcome to Phyllis—her grinning brother Ted!

The consternation of the guilty pair was almost ludicrous, at least Ted found it so. Then Phyllis recovered her self-possession and demanded:

"What are *you* doing here, I'd like to know?"

"Please, ma'am, that's a question I prefer to ask of you—and with a great deal more reason!" returned Ted. "Of all the nervy things I ever saw, it's you prowling around the Danforths' closed bungalow and sneaking out like a thief when you thought no one was around!" Leslie felt herself turn red and uncomfortable at the accusation, but Phyllis seemed in no wise daunted.

"I guess if I want to show the place to Leslie, there isn't any particular harm in it. She's been asking me what it looked like in there and how it differed from their house. You know perfectly well, the Danforths wouldn't care a brass farthing!" This statement happened to be entirely true, for Leslie *had* questioned her only the day before as to the interior arrangements and expressed some curiosity to see it. She breathed a sigh of relief at the ease with which Phyllis seemed to be explaining a rather peculiar situation.

Ted, however, seemed only half convinced. "If that's so, it's mighty queer that you looked so guilty and caught-in-the-act-y when you came out and saw me! And for goodness sake, how long have you been in there, anyway? This Rags dog came running up the beach to us at least an hour ago. And I thought, of course, you girls were somewhere about. But when you didn't appear after a while, I began to get worried, and Rags and I started off to find you. He led me straight here (good old chap!) and we've been sitting waiting at least fifteen minutes. Then he began to howl and gave the game away. Now please explain all this!"

"I'll explain nothing further," replied Phyllis, loftily, "and I'll trouble you to tend to your own affairs in the future!" With which crushing rejoinder she marched away, dragging the unhappy Leslie after her.

"All right! Just you wait! I'll dig out your little secret!" he called after them.

"And he will, too!" muttered Phyllis. "That is, if we don't use the greatest caution. Isn't it unfortunate that that wretched dog led him right here! However, I've settled him for the present, and now let's think about other things."

But it was not so easy for Leslie to forget the unpleasantness of the recent encounter and the implication that she had been caught trespassing. But Phyllis settled down to steady talk about their investigations and she presently forgot the impression.

"It's mighty strange that in all our careful search we didn't find a single thing that would indicate a recent visitor," mused Phyllis.

"Didn't you see anything—any *least* little thing?" questioned Leslie.

Phyllis stared at her in some surprise. "Why, you *know* I didn't! What makes you ask?"

"Because I *did*!" Leslie quietly returned.

CHAPTER VI

LESLIE MAKES SOME DEDUCTIONS

"Well, of all things!" ejaculated the astonished Phyllis. "And you never said a word! What was it?"

"I didn't say anything," explained Leslie, "because there was hardly a chance. It was just before we came out. And—"

"But what was it? Never mind how it happened!" cried Phyllis impatiently.

"Well, this is part of it. In that southwest bedroom (the one facing our house), I saw a tiny string of beads lying under the bureau, just by the front leg of it. The string was just a thread about three inches long, with some little green beads on it. A few of the beads had come off it and rolled farther away. I picked one of them up, and here it is." She held out a little bead to Phyllis.

"But what on earth is there to *this*?" exclaimed Phyllis, staring at it disappointedly. "I don't see what an insignificant little object like this proves. It was probably left by the Danforths, anyway."

"No, I don't think it was," returned Leslie, quietly, "because the Danforths seem to have cleaned the place very thoroughly. The rest of the floor was spick and span as could be. I think the string of beads was part of a fringe, such as they wear so much nowadays to trim nice dresses. It probably caught in the leg of that bureau and was pulled off without its owner realizing it. Now did any of the Danforths, as far as you know, have any bead-trimmed dresses that they wore down here?"

Phyllis shook her head. "I begin to see what you're driving at, Leslie. No, there's only Mrs. Danforth to wear dresses—the rest of the family consists of her husband and the boys. I'm perfectly certain I never saw her in a beaded dress. And even if she had one, I'm sure she wouldn't think of wearing it down here, not even to travel home in. People don't bring elaborate clothes to this place, and she's never been known to. I believe you're right. If the beads had been there when the place was cleaned, they would have disappeared. They must have come there since. The mysterious 'she' of the footprint must have left them! But what else was there?"

"Then I noticed another thing that was curious and very puzzling. I confess, I can't make much out of it, and yet it may mean a great deal. It was out by the fireplace in the living-room. Did you happen to notice that one of the bricks in the floor of it looked as if an attempt had been made to pry it loose, or something? The cement all along one side had been loosened and then packed down into place again. And 'way in the corner, I picked up *this*!" She held up the blade of a penknife, broken off halfway.

"No, I hadn't noticed it at all!" exclaimed Phyllis, ruefully. "The truth is, Leslie, I went into that place expecting to see it all torn up or upheaved or something of the kind—something very definite, anyway. And when I didn't find anything of the sort, I was awfully disappointed and hardly stopped to notice any of these small things. But I believe what you've found may be very important, and I think you're awfully clever to have noticed them, too. Why, it actually sounds like a regular detective story! And now that you've found these things, what do you make out of them? Have you any ideas?"

Leslie wrinkled her brows for an interval in silent thought. At last she said, "Yes, I have a good many ideas, but I haven't had time to get them into any order yet. They're all sort of—chaotic!"

"Oh, never mind!" cried the ever-impatient Phyllis. "Tell me them, anyway. I don't care how chaotic they are!"

"Well, to begin with,—has this occurred to you?—whoever comes here selects only a stormy, rainy night for a visit. Now *why*, unless they think it the best kind of time to escape observation. They just calculate on few people going out or even *looking* out of their houses on that kind of a night. Isn't that so?"

"It certainly seems to be," agreed Phyllis, "but what do you prove by that?"

"I don't *prove* anything, but I've drawn a conclusion from it that I'll tell you later. Then, there's the matter of this little bead. I know you rather scorned it when I first showed it to you, but do you realize one thing? We may be able to identify the owner by means of it."

Phyllis stared at her incredulously, but Leslie continued: "Yes, I really think so, and I'll tell you why. This isn't an ordinary bead. In the first place, it's a rather peculiar shade of green—one you don't ordinarily see. Then, though it's so small, it's cut in a different way, too, sort of melon-shaped, only with about six sides. Do you see?"

On closer examination, Phyllis did see. And she had to acknowledge that Leslie was right.

"Then there's the broken penknife and the brick with one side pried out," went on Leslie. "It's pretty plain that the person was trying to pry up that brick with the penknife and found it hard work because the mortar or cement is solid. Then the blade of the knife broke and the attempt was probably given up. Now why did they want to pry up that brick?"

"I know!—I know!" cried Phyllis, triumphantly. "They wanted to bury 'The Dragon's Secret' under it!"

"Maybe they did and maybe they didn't," replied Leslie, more cautiously. "They certainly tried to pry up the brick, but perhaps it was to *look* for something under it, rather than to hide anything. However, I rather think it was to hide it. And because they didn't succeed, they went out and buried it in the sand, instead. How about *that*?"

Phyllis sprang up and hugged her impetuously. "You have a brain like a regulation sleuth-hound's!" she laughed. "What else?"

"Well, this is what I can't understand. Suppose this person (we're sure now it must be a woman) came down here that first stormy night with 'The Dragon's Secret,' and tried to hide it somewhere, and finally buried it in the sand outside. The question is, what did she come for the *second* time?"

"To get it again?" suggested Phyllis.

"I'm almost absolutely certain not, because, if so, all she would have had to do was to go outside and dig. (Of course, she wouldn't have found it because we had it!) But she never went outside at all. I know that positively. I passed right by the place where Rags dug the hole, on my way up from your bungalow, and it was quite untouched, just as we left it after we filled it up again that day. And when we came back again, I looked a second time, and still it was the same. And I watched half the night and would certainly have seen if any one had gone there. No, I'm sure it wasn't for that. But what was it for?"

"Give it up," advised Phyllis, "at least for the present. Anything else?"

"No, except the conclusion I drew about the person's coming on a stormy night. Do you realize this?—there's quite a big chance that they—or rather, *she*!—will come again on the *next* stormy night—perhaps!"

"Well, if that's the case," exclaimed Phyllis, "I've drawn a little conclusion of my own. The next stormy night I'm going to spend at your bungalow—and we're going to keep awake all night!"

CHAPTER VII

A NEW DEVELOPMENT

But the weather remained quite clear for several nights after this. And meantime other things happened that gave a new twist to the girls' conjectures.

Two mornings after the events of the last chapter, Phyllis appeared at Rest Haven with a mysterious wrapped parcel in her hand. Answering Leslie's curious glance, she whispered:

"I want you to take this thing and keep it here and hide it. It's 'The Dragon's Secret.' I don't feel safe a minute with it around our place since Ted's performance the other day. You know, he boasted he'd find out our secret, and he will certainly make every effort to, or I don't know him. Whether he'll succeed or not depends upon how clever *we* are in spoiling his plans. If he found this, though, we might as well not try to keep the rest from him. I discovered him snooping around my room rather suspiciously yesterday. This was locked up in my trunk, and he *said* he was only hunting for fudge! But anyhow, you'd better keep it now, if you can think of some safe place to hide it."

"I'm sure I don't know where to put it!" sighed Leslie, rather worried by the responsibility. "Aunt Marcia and I shared one big trunk because it didn't seem worth while to bring two, when one needs so few things here. So of course I couldn't put it in there, and the lock of my suitcase is broken. There isn't a bureau-drawer with a key in the whole bungalow—so what am I going to do?"

For a time, Phyllis was equally puzzled. Then suddenly she had a bright idea. "I'll tell you! That top shelf in your pantry where the refrigerator is! You said you'd put quite a few kitchen things that you didn't use there, and it's dark and unhandy and neither your aunt nor any one else would think of disturbing it. Wouldn't that be the best place, really?"

"I guess you're right," admitted Leslie, considerably relieved. "Wait till Aunt Marcia has gone to sit on the front veranda, and we can put it there."

The Dragon's Secret had probably known some strange resting-places in its time, but doubtless none stranger than the one in which it now found itself—a dark, rather dusty top shelf in a pantry, hobnobbing with a few worn-out pots and pans and discarded kitchen-ware! But the girls tucked it far into a corner, and, wrapped in its burlap bag, it was as successfully concealed as it would have been in a strong-box.

"And now, there's something I've been wanting to ask you," said Leslie, as the two girls strolled down to the beach. "Do you happen to know anything about the people who hired Curlew's Nest the latter part of this summer?"

"Oh, yes!" answered Phyllis, "though I didn't happen to see them myself. Mrs. Danforth told me that in July the Remsons had it, as they always do. But in August and September she rented it to an elderly gentleman,—I can't think of his name, just this minute,—who stayed there all by himself, with only his man or valet to do all the work. He wasn't very well,—was recovering from some kind of a fever, I think,— and wanted to be alone in some quiet place. You know, Mrs. Danforth herself spent all summer in your bungalow, and she said she saw very little of the man in Curlew's Nest, though they were such near neighbors. He sat on his porch or in the house a great deal, or took long walks by himself on the beach. He used to pass the time of day with her, and make some other formal remarks, but that was about all. She was really rather curious about him, he seemed so anxious not to mix with other people or be talked to. But he left about the middle of September, and she closed up that bungalow for the winter. That's about all I know."

"It's too bad you can't think of his name!" exclaimed Leslie.

"Why?" demanded Phyllis, suddenly curious. "You surely don't think that has anything to do with *this* affair, do you?"

But Leslie countered that question by asking another: "Has it ever occurred to you as strange, Phyllis, that whoever got into that bungalow lately, knew the little secret about the side door and worked it so cleverly?"

Phyllis's eyes grew wide and she seized Leslie's arm in so muscular a grip that Leslie winced. "No, it didn't, you little pocket-edition *Sherlock Holmes*! But I see what you're driving at. To know about that side door, one must have been pretty well acquainted with that bungalow—*lived* in it for a while! Aha! No wonder you're curious about the last occupant. We'll have to count that old gentleman in on this!"

"Yes, but here's the mystery," reminded Leslie. "You said he lived here alone except for his man-servant. Remember, please, that the footprint we saw—was a *woman's*!"

Phyllis tore at her hair in mock despair. "Worse and more of it!" she groaned. "But the deeper it gets, the more determined I grow to get to the bottom of it!"

They strolled on a while in silence. Suddenly Phyllis asked, "Where's Rags this morning?"

"He doesn't seem to feel very well to-day. Something seems to have disagreed with him—perhaps too many hermit-crabs! Anyway, he's lying around on the veranda and seems to want to stay near Aunt Marcia and sleep. She said she'd keep him there."

"Best news I've heard in an age!" exclaimed Phyllis, delightedly. "That dog is a most faithful article, Leslie, but he's a decided nuisance sometimes! And now, I have a gorgeous idea that I've been wanting to try for two days. Father and Ted have gone off for the day up the inlet, and Rags is out of commission. Here's our chance. Do you realize that there's one bedroom in Curlew's Nest we didn't have a chance to explore the other day? Let's go and do it right now. I'll run down to our house for the electric torch and meet you at the side door. There's not a soul around to interfere with us!"

"Oh, no, Phyllis! I really don't think we ought—" objected Leslie, recalling all too vividly the unpleasantness of their former experience. But Phyllis was off and far away while she was still expostulating, and in the end, Leslie found herself awaiting her companion in the vicinity of the side door of Curlew's Nest.

They entered the dark bungalow with beating hearts, more aware this time than ever that mystery lurked in the depth of it. Straight to the unexplored bedroom they proceeded, for, as Leslie reminded them, they had no time to waste; Rags might have an untimely recovery and come seeking them as before! Ted also might be prompted by his evil genius to descend on them; or even Aunt Marcia might be minded to hunt them up.

The bedroom in question, as Phyllis now recalled, was the southwest one, and the one Mrs. Danforth said that the last tenant had chosen for his own. "Therefore it ought to be more than ordinarily interesting," went on Phyllis. "I remember now that Mrs. Danforth said he had asked permission to leave there, as a little contribution to the bungalow, a few books that he had finished with and did not wish to carry away. She left them right where they were on a shelf in his room, instead of putting them in the bookcase in the living-room. I'm sort of remembering these things she told me, piecemeal, because Mrs. Danforth is a great talker and is always giving you a lot of details about things you're not particularly interested in, and you try to listen politely, but often find it an awful bore. Then you try to forget it all as soon as possible!"

They found the bedroom in question somewhat more spacious and better furnished than the others. But though they examined every nook and cranny with care, they discovered nothing thrilling, or even enlightening, within its walls till they came to the shelf of books. These, with the exception of two books of recent fiction, were all of travel and politics in foreign countries.

"My, but he must have been interested in India and China and Tibet and those countries!" exclaimed Leslie, reading the titles. "I wonder why?"

She took one of them down and turned the pages idly. As she did so, something fluttered out and fell to the floor. "Oh!" she cried, picking it up and examining it. "Phyllis, this may prove very valuable! Do you see what it is?" It was an envelop of thin, foreign-looking paper—an empty envelop, forgotten and useless, unless perhaps it had been employed as a bookmark. But on it was a name—the name no doubt of the recipient of the letter it had once contained, and also a foreign address.

"Do you see what it says?" went on Leslie, excitedly. "'*Honorable Arthur Ramsay, Hotel des Wagons-Lits, Peking*'. Why, Phyllis, that's his name (which you couldn't remember!) and he was evidently at some time in Peking!"

But Phyllis was puckering her brows in an effort of memory. "There's some mistake here, I guess," she remarked at length, "for now I recall that Mrs. Danforth said his name was Mr. Horatio Gaines!"

Leslie dropped the envelop back in the book, the picture of disappointment. "It doesn't seem likely he'd have someone else's envelops in his books," she remarked. "And I think Honorable Arthur Ramsay of Peking sounds far more thrilling than plain 'Horatio Gaines'! Let's look through the rest of the books and see if we can discover anything else."

They examined them all, but found nothing more of interest and Leslie suggested uneasily that they had better go.

"But there's one thing I must see first,—" decided Phyllis; "the beads and broken penknife you found. I've been wild to look at them for myself. Come along! We'll have time for that."

They made their way cautiously into the next bedroom, bent down, and turned the torch toward the floor under the bureau where Leslie had made the discovery. Then both girls simultaneously gasped. There was not a sign of the beads anywhere to be seen!

"Phyllis!" breathed Leslie, in frightened wonder. "It's gone—the whole string! What can be the meaning of it?"

"Come!" cried Phyllis, dragging Leslie after her. "Let's go and see if the broken penknife blade is there yet. If that's gone, too, something new has happened here!"

They hurried to the living-room and bent over the fireplace. The half-loosened brick was there as Leslie had described it, but of the broken penknife blade in the corner, there was not a vestige to be seen!

CHAPTER VIII

THE CLUE OF THE GREEN BEAD

With shaking knees and blank dismay on their faces, they crept out of Curlew's Nest and fastened the door. Then they hurried down to the water's edge and sat on a rise of sand to talk it over.

"What can it all mean, Phyllis?" quavered Leslie.

"It means that some one has been in there again since day before yesterday," declared her companion, "though it's been bright moonlight for the past two nights, and how they got in without being seen, I can't quite understand! You said you kept some sort of watch, didn't you?"

"I certainly did. I haven't gone to bed till late, and every once in a while during the night, I've waked up and looked over there. It doesn't seem possible they would dare to come with the moonlight bright as day, all night long. Of course, that side door is on the opposite side from us, and the only way I could tell would be by seeing a light through the cracks of the shutter. Perhaps if they hadn't had a very bright light, I wouldn't know."

"But what did they come for?" questioned Phyllis.

"Why, that's simple. They came back to get the beads and the knife-blade. Probably it was the 'mysterious she,' and she came to get those things because she realized they'd been left there and might be discovered by some one else. What else could it be?"

"Of course you must be right," agreed Phyllis. "But it's the queerest thing I ever heard of! Anyway, there's *one* thing the lady doesn't know—that we have still one of the beads! I wonder how she'd feel if she *did* realize it?"

"Do you ever wonder what that mysterious lady is like?" asked Leslie. "I often try to picture her—from the very, very little we know about her. I think she is tall and dark and slender, and very, very stylishly dressed. She has rather sad brown eyes and is quite foreign-looking and would be very interesting to know."

"Well, I don't imagine her that way at all," replied Phyllis. "To me it seems as if she must be large and imposing, with light hair and blue eyes and very quick, vivacious manners. I agree that she is no doubt dressed in a very up-to-date style, and is probably about thirty-five or forty years old. I don't know whether I'd like to know her or not, but I *would* like to know what she's after in that bungalow!"

So they continued to conjecture and imagine till Phyllis finally exclaimed: "Why, there are Father and Ted back already! Fishing must have been poor this morning. Thank goodness we got out of that place when we did! But that reminds me, I ought to go to the village and order some supplies. The grocer doesn't come here again for two days. Don't you want to walk down with me? It's a gorgeous morning for a 'hike'!"

"I believe I will," agreed Leslie, "that is, if Aunt Marcia can get along without me. I haven't had a good walk in so long that I fairly ache for one. I'll go and see if Aunt Marcia would like me to get her anything, and I'll meet you in five minutes."

It was indeed a glorious morning for a walk. The crisp October air was as clear as crystal and the salt meadows back of the dunes were still gay with goldenrod and the deeper autumn colorings. The creek that wound through them was a ribbon of intense blue, and a thousand marsh-birds twittered and darted and swooped over its surface. But the two girls were, for once, almost blind to the beauty of it all, so absorbed were they in the never-failing topic of their mystery. And the village was reached almost before they realized they were in its vicinity.

Phyllis did her shopping first, in the general grocery store. Then Leslie suggested that they visit the little fancy-goods store and look up some wool for Miss Marcia's knitting. It was a very tiny little store, kept by a tiny, rather sleepy old lady, who took a long time to find the articles her customers required. It seemed as if she would never, never locate the box with the right shade of wool in it!

While they were waiting, not altogether patiently, a handsome automobile drew up in front of the store. Its only occupant was a young girl scarcely older than Leslie and Phyllis, and by the ease with which she handled the car, it was plain to be seen that she was an accomplished driver. In another moment she had entered the store and was standing beside the two girls, waiting to be served.

She was short and slender in build, with a pink-and-white complexion, of marvelous clearness,and fluffy, red-brown hair. Under the heavy coat which she had unbuttoned on entering the store could be seen a stylish suit of English tweeds, very tailor-made and up-to-date, and a smart tam crowned her red-brown hair.

After the pleasant manner of the villagers and accustomed summer people, Phyllis bade her "Good morning!" But, to the astonishment of both girls, instead of replying in an equally pleasant manner, she stared at them both up and down for a moment, then turned away with only an ungracious nod. The indignant pair left her severely alone after that, except for a furtive glance or two when she was looking the other way. But when they had at last ascertained that old Mrs. Selby had, after all, *no* wool of the shade required, Leslie hurried Phyllis out with what seemed almost unnecessary haste.

"The little wretch!" sputtered Phyllis, once safely outside. "Did you *ever* see worse manners? But she's—"

"Never mind about her manners!" whispered Leslie, excitedly. "Did you notice anything else?"

"Noticed that she was very smart looking and quite pretty—that is, I thought so at first. But after she acted that way, she seemed positively *hateful*!"

"No, no! I don't mean that. Did you notice anything about her dress—her clothes?"

"Oh, do tell me what you mean!" cried Phyllis. "How you do love to mystify a person!"

"Well," whispered Leslie, her eyes still on the door of the little store, "when she threw open her coat I just happened to glance at her dress, and noticed that it had a girdle of some dark green, crêpe-y material, and the two ends had fringes of beads— *and the beads were just like the ones in Curlew's Nest!*"

Phyllis simply stared at her, open-mouthed and incredulous. "It can't be!" she muttered at length. "Even if the beads were like the ones you found—there are probably more persons than one who have some like them."

"Yes, that's true," admitted Leslie, "but the color—and queer shape—everything!— At least, it's something worth investigating. It's the first real clue we've had."

At that moment, the girl in question came out of the store, sprang into the car, whirled the wheel about, and was off down the street in a cloud of dust. They stood gazing after her.

"It doesn't seem possible!" exclaimed Phyllis. "It just can't be! And yet—tell you what! I'm just wondering whether she's staying anywhere around here or is just a casual stranger passing through the town. Let's go in and ask old Mrs. Selby if she knows anything about her. If she's staying here, Mrs. Selby will positively know it. I'll make the excuse of having forgotten to buy something. Come along!

She hustled Leslie back into the little shop and soon had little Mrs. Selby hunting for a size and variety of shell hair-pin of which she had no need whatever, as she possessed already a plentiful supply at home. But it was the only thing she could think of at the moment. When they were being wrapped, she asked quite casually:

"Was that young girl who just went out a stranger here, Mrs. Selby, or is she stopping in the village? Seems to me I don't recall her face."

"Oh, she ain't exactly a stranger," replied Mrs. Selby with alacrity, quite waking up at the prospect of retailing a bit of gossip; "But she ain't been around here so long—only a couple of weeks or so. She comes in here once in a while, but she ain't very friendly like—never passes the time o' day nor nothing,—just asks for what she wants and goes out. I never did quite take to manners like that. Nobody else here acts so—not even the summer folks. I can't think how she was brung up! They do say as she ain't an American,—that she's English or something,—but I don't know for sure. Anyhow, she don't mix with no one—just runs around in that ottymobile all the time."

"Where's she stopping?" went on Phyllis. "The hotel is closed. I thought all the summer people but ourselves had gone."

"Oh, she's boarding up to Aunt Sally Blake's. I dunno how she come to go there, but there she is. I wonder how Aunt Sally gets along with her?"

"Have you heard what her name is?" pursued Phyllis, as she received her parcel.

"They do say her name is Ramsay—Miss Ramsay. Good morning, young ladies, and thank you. Come in again soon."

When they were out on the street, Leslie clutched Phyllis spasmodically and her eyes were almost popping out of her head.

"Is there the least doubt in your mind *now*, Phyllis Kelvin?" she demanded. "Her name is Ramsay—the very same name that was on the envelop in the book!"

And Phyllis was obliged to acknowledge herself convinced.

CHAPTER IX

AUNT SALLY ADDS TO THE MYSTIFICATION

THE two girls walked home in a state bordering on stupefaction. Every little while Phyllis would stop to ejaculate: "Who would have thought it! The horrid little snob! I really can't believe yet that it is she, Leslie—our 'mysterious she!' I'm sure there must be some mistake."

"Well, of course, it *may* not be so," Leslie admitted, "but you must see how many things point to it. The beads are identical. I stood so near her that I had a fine chance to see them closely. Her name is the same as the one on the envelop in the book—"

"Yes, but that isn't the name of the man who hired the bungalow," objected Phyllis.

"That's quite true, but even so, you can't tell what connection there may be with the other name. It isn't exactly a common one, and that makes it all the more likely that we may be right. And then, there's the fact of her being so near here—right in the village. I have always imagined that whoever it was had to come from quite a distance, and I've always wondered how she managed it, so late at night."

"But Leslie, why on earth should she come to that bungalow in the dead of night, in a storm, and hide that 'Dragon's Secret'? What mysterious affair can she be mixed up with, anyway?"

Leslie, however, had no solution to offer to this poser, but she did have a sudden idea that made her stop short in the road and gasp:

"Do you realize, Phyllis Kelvin, that we are doing a very questionable—yes, a *wrong* thing in keeping the 'Dragon's Secret,' when it evidently belongs to this girl?"

"How do you *know* it belongs to this girl?" countered Phyllis. "You only *guess* that it may, when all's said and done. You didn't see her hide it there—you didn't even see *her* at the bungalow. We may be way off the track, for all you know, and we'd be a pretty pair of geese to go and meekly hand it to her, shouldn't we! And do you know, even if I was simply *positive* it was hers, I just wouldn't give it to her, anyway, for a while. I'd let her stew and fret for it for a good long spell—after such hatefulness!"

Phyllis's manner was so vindictive that Leslie had to smile in spite of herself.

"But oh, see here!" Phyllis went on. "*I* have an idea—a glorious idea! It may help to clear up a lot of things. I know Aunt Sally Blake very well, and we'll go and see her—this very afternoon! Perhaps she can give us more light on the subject."

"But wouldn't that seem too plainly like tracking down this—Miss Ramsay?" objected Leslie, "especially as she doesn't appear to care for our acquaintance!"

"Not a bit!" declared Phyllis, positively. "You don't realize how well *I* know Aunt Sally. Why, she's a regular village institution—everybody knows her and thinks the world of her. She's a plump, jolly, delightful old lady who lives in a delightful old house full of dear, old-fashioned furniture. She keeps a lot of chickens and often sells them and the fresh eggs, and she does a little sewing, and sometimes takes a boarder or two, and goes out nursing occasionally—and oh, I don't know what all! But I know that we couldn't get along at all around here without Aunt Sally. We'll go down to her house this afternoon and call (I really haven't been to see her since I came down this time), and I'll ask her if she has a nice roasting chicken that I can have. That'll be a perfectly good excuse. And if our polite young lady isn't around, I'll try and get her to talk. Aunt Sally loves to talk, but she isn't a gossip like old Mrs. Selby, and we'll have to go at it a little more carefully."

They solaced themselves with this thought, and awaited with more than a little impatience the visit that afternoon. Surely Aunt Sally, if any one, would be able to solve some of their mysteries!

By afternoon, the weather had turned warm, almost sultry, and they found Aunt Sally sitting on her front porch, rocking gently and humming to herself over her sewing. She was delighted to see Phyllis again and to make the acquaintance of Leslie, whom Phyllis introduced as her neighbor and very dear friend. When they had chatted about topics of common interest for a while, Phyllis introduced the subject of the chicken.

"Bless your heart, dear!" cried Aunt Sally. "I'm so sorry, but I haven't a roasting chicken just now in the whole yard—nothing but fowls. But I can give you a couple of nice young broilers—and I've plenty of fresh eggs."

Phyllis straightway arranged to have two broilers ready for her when she called for them next day, and skilfully changed the subject.

"Oh, Aunt Sally! do show Leslie those begonias you've been raising all summer. I do think they are the most beautiful things! You certainly are very successful at making things grow!"

Highly flattered, Aunt Sally rose to lead the girls indoors to the sunny room where she kept her plants. While they were admiring them, she asked them to sit down and rest a while and talk—an invitation they accepted with great alacrity. At length, after a detailed account of the health and affairs of her entire family, Phyllis craftily led the conversation back to Aunt Sally herself.

"And are you alone now, Aunt Sally, or is your sister still with you? I heard she was going back to Ohio."

"Yes, she's gone and I'm alone," sighed Aunt Sally; "at least,—I'm not quite alone. I have a boarder at present."

"Oh, *have* you!" exclaimed Phyllis, guilefully, as if it were all news to her. "Why, that's very nice. I hope the boarder will stay a long while. It will be some company for you."

"Well, I dunno how long she'll stay, and she ain't much company for *me*, I must confess!" admitted Aunt Sally, with a somewhat worried air. "The truth is, I can't exactly make her out."

This was precisely the line that Phyllis wished her to take, yet even now caution must be observed or Aunt Sally might shy away from it.

"Oh, it's a lady then!" remarked the artful Phyllis.

"Well, no, it ain't exactly a lady—it's a young girl 'bout the age of you two, I should guess."

"Still, I don't see why she shouldn't be company for you, even so," argued Phyllis, quite as if she were still completely in the dark as to this new boarder.

"The reason she ain't much company," went on Aunt Sally, "is because—well, I don't know as I ought to say it, but I guess she thinks she's too sort of—high-toned to 'sociate with the person who keeps her boarding-house!" Aunt Sally laughed, an amused, throaty little chuckle at this, and then the worried frown came back.

"Why, she must be rather horrid, I think," commented Phyllis, with more heartfelt reason than Aunt Sally could guess!

"No, I don't think she means to be horrid—she's just been brought up that way, I guess. I wish she could be more friendly. I sort of feel a responsibility about her. You see, she's here all alone. She was staying at the hotel with her grandfather, and he suddenly took awful sick and had to be taken to the hospital up at Branchville. She stayed on at the hotel so's to be near him (she runs up there every day in her car), and then the hotel had to close down for the season. The manager come to me and asked me if I could take her in, 'cause he was kind of sorry for her, her grandfather bein' so ill, an' she couldn't seem to find no other place. So I did, but she worries me a lot, somehow. I don't like to see a young girl like that with no one to look after her, and she running around loose in that auto all the time. Why, she even took it out one rainy night last week at ten o'clock. Said she was worried about her grandfather, but I didn't approve of her running all the way up there to Branchville in the rain."

Here Phyllis glanced significantly at Leslie and interjected a question. "Did she and her grandfather have one of the bungalows on the beach this summer, do you know, Aunt Sally?"

"Why, not that I know of. She said she'd been visiting some friends somewhere in Maine, and then come on here to join her grandfather just a few days before he was taken sick. I don't think it likely she ever stayed in one of the bungalows. She didn't seem to know anything about this region at first. And I'd likely have heard of it if she had. But, laws! I got biscuits in the oven and I'm clean forgetting them!" And with a whisk of skirts, Aunt Sally vanished for a moment into the kitchen.

"What did I tell you!" whispered Leslie. "Went out in the rain one night last week about ten o'clock! I warrant she didn't go to the hospital, or, if she did, it was after she'd visited Curlew's Nest!"

But Aunt Sally was back almost immediately, bearing some hot biscuits and jam which she hospitably invited her guests to try. And while they were partaking of this refreshment she sighed:

"My, how I have been gossiping about that poor girl! I sort of feel conscience-stricken, for I could like her real well if she'd only let me. She's a sort of lovable-looking child! I wish she knew you two girls. I believe it would do her a lot of good to be around with you. There she is now!"—she cried, as a car flashed past the window and up the driveway toward the barn. "Just wait till she comes in and I'll introduce you—"

"No, no!" exclaimed Phyllis, hastily springing up. "Better not, Aunt Sally. If she doesn't care for you, I'm sure she wouldn't for us. Besides, we must go right away. Remember, we're both the *cooks* in our families, and even as it is, we won't be back very early. It's a long walk. Good-by, and thank you, and I'll send for the broilers to-morrow!" And with Leslie in tow, she hurried away, leaving a somewhat bewildered Aunt Sally gazing after them.

"Well, I guess not! The idea of trying to get acquainted a second time with that difficult young person!" Phyllis exploded, when they were out of ear-shot.

"And yet," mused Leslie as they swung along, "unpleasant as the thought of it is, I wonder if it wouldn't be a good idea—to get acquainted?"

CHAPTER X

AT DAWN

"How do you mean—it might be the best thing to get acquainted with her?" demanded Phyllis, indignantly.

"Why, if we could do so in some way that wasn't like forcing ourselves on her, it might lead to a good many things—solving our mystery mainly. And then,—who knows?—she *might* be pleasant when you come to know her better."

"No chance!" declared Phyllis, and dismissed that subject. "Well, Aunt Sally didn't do much toward clearing up things, did she?" she went on. "I was in hopes she'd be able to give us a good many more ideas. One thing's certain though. That girl evidently came here in the car that rainy night, but—Look here! Something strange has just occurred to me—Aunt Sally didn't say *which* rainy night, and there have been two in the past ten days. I judge that the girl must have been with her for at least a couple of weeks, for the hotel closed up more than two weeks ago."

"I've been thinking of that, too," replied Leslie. "And, do you know, I'm almost certain Aunt Sally must have meant the *last* one, because she only said *'rainy'* night. If she'd meant that other, wouldn't she have said 'the night of the hard storm,' or something like that? Because it really *was* unusual, and if this Miss Ramsay had gone out *that* night, I believe Aunt Sally would have been considerably more shocked and would have said so. What do you make of it?"

"The only thing I can make out of it is that she didn't go out that first night. But if she *didn't* visit Curlew's Nest that night, then who in the world *did*?"

This certainly was a poser, and neither of the two girls could find an adequate conjecture that would answer.

"Then, this Horatio Gaines who hired the bungalow must be her grandfather. Of course, the *name* is different, but he may be the grandfather on her mother's side. But if that is the case, who is the 'Hon. Arthur Ramsay'?" questioned Phyllis.

"Perhaps her father or her other grandfather," ventured Leslie.

"That's possible; but I wish I had found out from Aunt Sally if she knew the name of the grandfather who is ill. That might explain something. I wish I had asked her at the time. I believe I'll go for the broilers myself to-morrow and see if I can find out any more in some way that won't make her suspect," declared Phyllis.

The next morning Phyllis was as good as her word. She went down to the village alone, as Leslie had matters that kept her at home that day. But she came flying back breathless, to impart her news.

"I managed to lead the conversation around—to that grandfather business—again," panted Phyllis, to Leslie, when she had induced her chum to come down to the beach for a moment, "and what do you think she said? That his name was *'Ramsay'!* Now what do you make of *that?* If his name is Ramsay, he can't be the man who hired that bungalow—and we're all on the wrong track!"

"No, it doesn't prove that at all," insisted Leslie. "The one who rented the bungalow, no matter what his name was, certainly had an envelop in his possession addressed to*Ramsay.* So you see there's a connection somewhere!"

Phyllis had to admit that this was so. "But here's something else stranger than that—what do you think of my having been introduced to and becoming acquainted with our 'exclusive young friend'?"

Leslie certainly opened her eyes in astonishment. "You're surely joking!" she exclaimed.

"No, positive truth! It happened this way: I was just about to leave with my chickens under my arm, when in walks this precious Miss Ramsay, right into the room. I could see she was prepared to turn on that cold stare effect again, but I never so much as noticed her existence. And then Aunt Sally bustled in,—she'd been upstairs a minute,—and blest if she didn't introduce us after all! Said the most complimentary things about yours truly, and how I was staying at my bungalow on the beach; and then she mentioned you, too, and told about you being in the 'Rest Haven' bungalow. It struck me that our young lady sort of pricked up her ears at that (though it *may* have been only imagination). But she just said 'How-de-do,' rather carelessly—didn't offer to shake hands or anything.

"I muttered something about it being a pleasant day and hoping she was enjoying the place. But she only replied, 'Oh, ya-as, thanks!' with that awfully English accent, and walked out of the room. Well, anyhow, we're formally acquainted now (whether either one of us enjoy it or not!), and that may be a useful thing later, perhaps."

It was still dark the next morning when Leslie awoke from a dreamless sleep—awoke suddenly, with the distinct impression that something unusual was happening.

She lay perfectly still for several moments, trying to localize the sensation more definitely. In her room were two windows—a small one facing Curlew's Nest and a large, broad one facing the sea. Leslie always had this window wide open, and her bed was so placed that she could easily look out of it.

She did so now, and noticed the first light streak of dawn along the east, and a brilliant star so close to the horizon that it seemed to be resting on the edge of the tossing ocean. Then her heart leaped and felt as if it almost turned over—for between her and the light, at the window, she descried the shape of a dark head!

Involuntarily Leslie sprang up to a sitting position. Then the tension relaxed and she drew a deep breath of relief. It was only Rags, standing on his hind legs at the window, his great shaggy head silhouetted against the light. In another instant he had uttered his low, rumbling growl of uneasiness.

"What is it, Rags? What do you see?" she called softly to him. He forsook the window for a moment and trotted over to nuzzle his head on her pillow, but almost immediately hurried back to his post at the window.

"There's something worrying him!" she thought. "Now I wonder what it can be. Suppose—suppose it were some one around that other bungalow again! I'd better get up and see."

She rose softly, slipped on a warm dressing-gown and slippers, and peered first out of the side window at Curlew's Nest. But the darkness was still intense on this side, there was no tell-tale light in the chinks of the shutters, and she was forced, after watching for several moments, to conclude that nothing was amiss in this region.

Then she went to the window facing the ocean, pushed Rags aside a trifle, and cuddled down beside him on the window-seat. The dawn was growing every moment brighter. The streak of gray along the horizon had grown to a broad belt of pink, and very faintly the objects on the beach were beginning to be visible. Rags still rumbled his uneasy growl at intervals, and stared intently at something Leslie's eye could not yet discern.

It was only by following the direction of his gaze that she presently realized there was something moving on the beach somewhere in front of Curlew's Nest. Then her heart actually did seem to stop beating for an instant, for in the growing light she at last could distinguish a dark form moving stealthily about by the old log where Rags had dug up the "Dragon's Secret!"

"Oh! who can it be? And what are they doing there?" she whispered distractedly to Rags. The dog's only reply was to growl a little louder, and she promptly silenced him.

"Be a good dog, Rags! Don't make a sound! It will rouse Aunt Marcia, and besides I *must* see who is there, if possible!" Rags settled down again to a quieter watch with evident reluctance.

With every passing moment, day was approaching nearer, and the scene out over the ocean was one of surprising beauty, had Leslie only been less occupied and had time to observe it. The band of pink had melted into gold, and a thousand rosy little clouds dimpled the sky above. It was now so light that the dark shape on the beach stood out with comparative clearness. It had been bending down and rising up at intervals, and it took little guessing on Leslie's part to conjecture what was happening. Some one was digging in the spot where the "Dragon's Secret" had been hidden!

"What if it is Miss Ramsay?" thought Leslie. "Oh, it *must* be she! Who else could it be? She's looking for that box, and she can't find it because we've taken it away. Oh, what ought I to do about it? If only Phyllis were here!"

At this moment she realized from the actions of the unknown person that the search was evidently abandoned. The figure stood upright, struck its hands together, and threw away some implement like a board, with which the digging had been done. Then, with a discouraged shrug of the shoulders and a hasty glance back at the two cottages, it turned and walked away down the beach and was shortly out of sight.

And it was then that Leslie sank back on the window seat with a little gasp of sheer astonishment.

The figure was not—*could* not have been that of Miss Ramsay! It was a *man*—a tall, burly man; and as he walked away, his gait gave evidence of a decided limp!

CHAPTER XI

AN UNEXPECTED VISITOR

So anxious was Leslie to impart this newest development to Phyllis that morning, that she ate no breakfast at all, a departure which worried Miss Marcia not a little. But Leslie was out of the house and off the moment she had finished washing the dishes.

It was some time before she could locate her companion, as the Kelvins had gone off early on a fishing expedition a short way up the inlet, having persuaded Phyllis to join them, a thing she had done but little of late. After a long walk and much halloo-ing, however, Leslie sighted their boat. And it took considerable time before she could persuade Phyllis to come ashore, as she could not very well impart to her, standing on the bank, that she had news of vital importance concerning their secret.

When Phyllis had at last been lured ashore and the two had walked away out of sight, she told the tale of her curious experience at dawn.

"And now, Phyllis, what do you make of it?" she demanded, wide eyed.

"There's only one thing to make of it," returned Phyllis, gravely, "And that is— there's some one else mixed up in this—some one we haven't known about or counted on at all! I thought Miss Ramsay, all along, was the only one concerned in it. Now we can only guess that that isn't so. But how to make head or tail of the whole thing is beyond me. What kind of a man did you say he was?"

Leslie described him again. "Of course, it was still hardly light and I couldn't see him plainly at all," she ended. "I never even got a glimpse of his face, nor how he was dressed. But he was tall and broad-shouldered, and I think stooped a little and walked with quite a decided limp."

"That last fact ought to help to identify him, if nothing else," mused Phyllis. "But I confess I'm more at sea than ever about the whole thing. I was beginning to think I'd reduced things to some kind of a theory, but this upsets everything. And it annoys me so to think I'm always out of it, being so far away from Curlew's Nest. I do believe I'll have to come and spend my nights with you or I'll never be on the scene of action at the most interesting time!"

"Oh, I *do* wish you would!" urged Leslie, earnestly. "I'm really beginning to be quite nervous about all this. It's so uncanny, not being able to say a word about it to Aunt Marcia or any one—being all alone there, or as good as alone, when these queer things happen. Don't you suppose we could arrange it somehow that you could come over and stay with me—without having it seem odd or out of the way to the others?"

They both thought hard over the problem for a moment. Suddenly Phyllis cried,—"I have it—I think! I heard Father and Ted planning to-day to be off fishing to-night, and as many nights after as the conditions are good. They just adore that kind of thing and have done very little of it this time. As a rule, I don't mind a bit staying alone at the bungalow if I don't happen to go with them. But I've never before had the excuse of having you here to be with. It will seem perfectly natural for me to say that, as they're to be away, I'll spend the night with you. How's that?"

"Oh, just the thing!" exclaimed Leslie, enthusiastically. "And now let's go back and take a swim. It's fairly mild and the best time of day for it. You left your suit at our house last time, so it's very convenient. You won't have to walk all the way back to your place."

They strolled back to Rest Haven in a leisurely fashion and had just turned the corner of the house and come in sight of the front veranda, when what they saw there almost took them off their feet. On the veranda sat Aunt Marcia, rocking comfortably back and forth, and opposite her, in another rocker sat—could their eyes have deceived them?—who but the redoubtable *Miss Ramsay!*

She was dressed as they had seen her in the village store, and she was chatting, with an appearance of the greatest affability, with Miss Marcia. The two girls stared at her in ill-concealed amazement—so ill-concealed, in fact, that even Miss Marcia noticed it.

"Miss Ramsay and I have been getting acquainted while we waited for you to come back," she remarked, somewhat bewildered by their speechless consternation. "She says she made your acquaintance at Aunt Sally Blake's in the village, where she is boarding."

"Oh—er, yes!" stuttered Phyllis, remembering her manners. "It's very pleasant to see you here, Miss—Ramsay. I see you are acquainted with Miss Crane. This is Miss Leslie Crane her niece."

Leslie bowed and murmured something inarticulate, but Miss Ramsay was affable to a degree. "I drove over to your cottage first, Miss Kelvin," she chatted on, after her introduction, "with some eggs Aunt Sally promised you. She was going to send them by the butcher boy, but he did not stop this morning, so, as I was going out, I offered to take them. But I found no one at your place, so I came on here, introduced myself to Miss Crane, and we've been having a nice time together."

The astonishment of the girls at this amazing change of front in the difficult Miss Ramsay was beyond all expression. Her intonation was slightly English, her manner charming. They had not dreamed that she could be so attractive. And so fresh and pretty was she that she was a real delight to look upon.

"What delightful little cottages these are!" she went on. "They look so attractive from the outside. I'm sure they must be equally so from the inside. We have nothing quite on this style in England, where I came from."

"Wouldn't you like to go through ours?" asked Miss Marcia, hospitably. "Leslie, take Miss Ramsay through. Perhaps she will be interested to see the interior."

"Oh, I'll be delighted!" exclaimed Miss Ramsay, and rose to accompany Leslie.

It did not take them long to make the round of Rest Haven. Rather to her hostess's astonishment, the girl seemed more enthusiastic over Leslie's room than any of the others and lingered there the longest, though it was by no means the most attractive.

"What a wonderful view you have of the sea!" she said. And then she strolled to the other window and looked out, long and curiously. "That's an interesting little cottage next door," she remarked presently. "Is it—is it just like this one?"

"Why no. It's larger and differently arranged and furnished more elaborately, too, I— I believe," faltered Leslie, hoping she had not appeared to know too much about it.

"I wonder if we could go through it?" went on the visitor. "I—I just love to see what these little seashore places look like. They're so different from ours."

"Oh, I hardly think so!" cried Leslie. "You see it's all locked up for the winter, and Mrs. Danforth, who owns it, has the key."

The girl looked at her intently. "And there's no other way, I suppose, beside the front door?"

"How should I know?" countered Leslie, suddenly on her guard. "If there *were* would it be right to try it, do you think? Wouldn't it be too much like trespassing?"

"Oh, of course!" laughed Miss Ramsay. "I only meant that it would be fun to look it over, if there were any proper way of doing so. You see, Grandfather and I might be here another summer and I'd just love to rent a little cottage like either one of these two."

She turned away from the window and they sauntered out of the room and back to the veranda.

"And now that you've seen Leslie's bungalow, you must run over and see ours, especially as it was at ours you at first intended to call!" said Phyllis. "Come along, Leslie, and we'll show Miss Ramsay over Fisherman's Luck!"

It struck the girls that Miss Ramsay showed a trifle less enthusiasm about returning to the other cottage. Still, she agreed, with a fair assumption of polite interest, and they tramped back along the beach, chatting agreeably.

But she showed very genuine pleasure in the entirely different appearance of Phyllis's abode, and a large surprise at the presence of a grand piano in so unusual a place. And when Leslie had informed her of Phyllis's talent she eagerly demanded that they be given an immediate concert.

And it was Phyllis's sudden whim to render a very charming and touching program, ending with the Chopin "Berceuse." The music died away in a hushed chord, and Leslie, who had been gazing out at the ocean during its rendering, was astonished when she looked around to see the visitor furtively wiping away a few tears.

"I'm a perfect goose about some kinds of music!" she muttered apologetically, and then, abruptly, "Won't you two girls please call me Eileen? I'm so lonely here and I haven't any friends and—and—I'd like to see you often."

And then the impulsive Phyllis put a comradely arm about her shoulder. "Just come as often as you like. We'll always be delighted to see you. I'm sure we three can have a jolly time together. And be sure to call us by our first names, too."

"Thank you, Phyllis and Leslie," she said simply. "You are more than kind to me. But I must be getting back now. It's most time for me to go to the hospital to see Grandfather. He's *so* ill, and I'm so worried about him!" Again the tears came into her eyes. "But good-by! I'm coming over to-morrow with the car to take you all out for a spin!" And she was gone, running down the path to where she had parked the car.

When they were alone, the two girls looked at one another.

"It's the most amazing thing I ever heard of—this change in her!" marveled Phyllis. "Have you the slightest idea what has caused it?"

"I think I have," answered Leslie, and she told of the girl's curious conduct when she was being shown through Rest Haven. "I believe she had a purpose in coming here—she may have thought she could find out something from us. And she certainly thought she might get into Curlew's Nest, though I don't believe for a minute the reason she gave was the only one. I think she didn't particularly want to go to see your place, either, but when she got here she liked it."

"Yes, and I like her—strange as you may think it!" declared Phyllis. "I've quite changed my mind about her. Do you know, I think that girl is having a whole lot of trouble, somehow or other—trouble she can't tell us about. What the mystery is and how it is connected with that cottage, I don't see. But I do believe that she likes *us*, and if we're ever going to solve this mystery at all, it will probably be through her."

"Shall we—do you think we ought to—give her the Dragon's Secret?" faltered Leslie.

"I certainly do *not*—at least not yet! I'll wait till I know a few things more before I make a move like that!" declared the emphatic Phyllis. "And now come along and let's have our swim."

CHAPTER XII
THE CURIOUS BEHAVIOR OF TED

True to their previous arrangement, Phyllis spent the night with Leslie at Rest Haven. They read together till a very late hour and then sat up even later, in the dark, watching from Leslie's window to see if there were any further developments at Curlew's Nest. But nothing unusual happened.

"Isn't that exactly my luck!" complained Phyllis. "If I weren't here, I suppose there'd be a half a dozen spooky visitors!"

"Oh, no!" laughed Leslie. "Probably nothing will happen again for some time. Remember how very few times it *has* happened, anyway. But it is provoking—just when we're all ready for it!"

"Do you know," exclaimed Phyllis suddenly, "this is the time when I'd just love to go through that place again! What do you say if we get out of this window and try it?"

"Oh, no, no!" cried Leslie. "You mustn't think of such a thing! Can't you see how awfully dangerous it would be? Just suppose some one should take it into their heads to visit the place again to-night—and find us in there. It would be a terrible position for us!"

"I wouldn't be afraid of Eileen!" stoutly declared Phyllis. "I'd rather enjoy meeting her there. It would give her something to explain!"

"But there's some one else you might meet there who might not be so amusing—the man with the limp!" Leslie reminded her.

Phyllis had to acknowledge that this was so, and the subject was dropped, much to Leslie's relief.

Next afternoon, Eileen came over with her car and invited the girls and Miss Marcia to go for a long ride. They all accepted with alacrity, enjoying the prospect of a change. Eileen insisted that Miss Marcia sit by her while she drove. And as she did this with remarkable ease, she was able to converse pleasantly with her guests most of the time. She took them for a very long drive, and they were all astonished at her familiarity with the roads in that part of the country. She assured them that she had grown to know them well, during the long days lately when she had little else to do than to explore them with the car.

It was dusk when they returned at last to the beach, and, having deposited Phyllis first at her bungalow, Eileen drove the others to theirs. They bade her good night at the foot of the wooden path that led up the slope to their cottage, and she sat and watched them, without starting the car, till they had disappeared indoors. But it so happened that Leslie turned around, opened the door, and came out again almost at once to get an armful of wood for the fire from the bin on the back veranda. And in so doing, it happened also that she witnessed a curious little incident.

Eileen seemed to have had a slight difficulty in starting the car, but it was in motion now, going slowly, and had advanced only about as far as the path leading up to Curlew's Nest. Leslie stood in the darkness of her porch, idly watching its progress, when something that happened caused her heart to leap into her throat. Out from some thick bushes at the edge of the road, there appeared a dark form, which signaled to the car. Eileen whirled the wheel around, applied the brake, and the car almost came to a stop. Almost—but not quite, for the figure leaped into it while it was still going. Then Eileen stepped on the accelerator, the car shot forward, and was almost instantly out of sight.

Eileen whirled the wheel around, applied the brake, and the car almost came to a stop

Leslie got her wood and went indoors in a daze. What could it all mean? What duplicity had Eileen been guilty of now? The thing certainly looked very, very sinister, consider it how you would! And she could breathe no word of it to her aunt, who, as Leslie entered, straightway began on a long eulogy of Eileen, her delightful manners, her thoughtfulness, and her kindness in giving them an afternoon of such enjoyment. It seemed to Leslie, considering what had just happened, that she must certainly scream with nervousness if Miss Marcia did not stop, and she tried vainly several times to steer her to another theme. But Miss Marcia had found a topic that interested her, and she was not to be diverted from it till it was exhausted!

With all her strength, Leslie longed for the time to come when Phyllis should appear, for she had promised to come again for the night. And when the supper was eaten and the dishes had been disposed of, Leslie went outside and paced and paced back and forth on the front veranda, peering vainly into the darkness to watch for her friend. Miss Marcia, indoors with Rags by the blazing fire, called several times to her to come in and share the warmth and comfort, but she felt she could not endure the confinement in the house and the peaceful sitting by the hearth, when her thoughts were so upset. Would Phyllis never appear? What could be keeping her?

It was a small, but very active, indignation meeting that was held when the two girls were at last together. Leslie would not permit Phyllis to go indoors for a time after she arrived, though the night was rather chilly, but kept her on the veranda to explain what had happened.

"The deceitful little thing!" cried Phyllis. "Now I see exactly what she took us all out for this afternoon, even Miss Marcia—to get rid of us all for a good long time while some accomplice of hers did what they pleased in Curlew's Nest, quite undisturbed by any one around!"

"That's exactly what it must have been," agreed Leslie. "But who could that other person have been?"

"The man with the limp?" suggested Phyllis.

"No, I'm very sure it was not he. This person sprang into the car while it was still in motion—was very active, evidently. I'm certain the man with the limp could never have done that!"

"Well, was it a man or a woman? Surely you could tell *that*!"

"No, actually I couldn't. It was getting so dark, and the figure was so far off, and it all happened so quickly that I couldn't see. But, Phyllis, I'm horribly disappointed in Eileen! I had begun to think she was lovely, and that we had misjudged her badly. And now—*this*!"

"She's simply *using* us—that's plain," agreed Phyllis. "She evidently intended to do so from the first, after she found out we were right on the spot here. She deliberately came out to cultivate our acquaintance and make it seem natural for her to be around here. Then she and the one she's working with planned to get us away from here for the whole afternoon and have the field free for anything they pleased. Faugh! It makes me sick to think of being duped like that!"

"But after yesterday—and the way she acted when you played Chopin, and what she said about our friendship, and all that—Was *anything* genuine at all?"

"Not a thing!" declared Phyllis, positively. "All put on to get a little farther into our good graces. Well, I'll never be caught like *that* again. We'll continue to seem very friendly to Miss Eileen Ramsay, but we won't be caught twice!"

"By the way, what made you so late to-night?" questioned Leslie, suddenly changing the subject. "I thought you'd never come!"

"Oh, I meant to tell you right away, but all this put it out of my head. When I got home after the ride, I found only Father there. He said Ted had been away most of the afternoon. He'd gone down to the village after some new fishing-tackle and hadn't come back yet. I started in and got supper, and still he didn't appear. Then we began to get worried and 'phoned down to Smithson's in the village where they sell tackle, to see if he could be there. They said he *had* been, early in the afternoon, but they hadn't seen him since. We called up every other place he could possibly be, but nowhere was he to be found. I was beginning to be quite upset about him—when in he walked!

"He was very quiet and uncommunicative and wouldn't explain why he was so late. And then, presently, he said in a very casual manner that his hand was hurt. And when he showed it to us, I almost screamed, for it was very badly hurt—all torn and lacerated. He had it wrapped in his handkerchief, but we made him undo it, and I bathed it and Fatherput iodine on, and I fixed him a sling to wear it in. The thing about it was that he didn't seem to want to tell us how it happened. Said he met a friend who invited him to ride in their car and had taken him for a long drive. And on the way home they'd had a little breakdown, and Ted had tried to help fix it and had got his hand caught in the machinery somehow.

"But he was plainly very anxious not to be questioned about it. And Father says that Ted is old enough now to be trusted, and should not be compelled to speak when he doesn't wish to, and so nothing more was said. But it all seemed a little strange to me, for, honestly, I don't know a single soul in this village that Ted knows who owns a car, or any other of our friends who would be likely to be around these parts just now.

They're all home at their schools or colleges. When I asked him whose car he was in, he just glared at me and said I always did ask too many impertinent questions! But I can't make much out of it, and I hate any more puzzles to think about."

Leslie, however, could cast no light on this new problem; and she was somewhat more interested, moreover, in their other puzzle. But as she was about to revert to that subject again, Phyllis suddenly interrupted:

"Oh, by the way, soon after I got home, Aunt Sally 'phoned to ask if we were back from the ride yet. And when I said we'd been back some time, she said she was quite worried because Eileen had not yet appeared and it was late and dark. I said perhaps she had stopped somewhere in the village, as she had left us a good while before. Quite a little later, just before Ted got in, Aunt Sally 'phoned again to say that Eileen had just arrived. She'd had some trouble with the car after she left us and had to stop and fix it. I wonder what was the matter *there*!"

Suddenly Leslie clutched her friend's arm. "Phyllis Kelvin, are we going crazy, or is there some strange connection in all this? Can't you see?—Ted late and mixed up with some breakdown—Eileen late and had trouble with the machinery,—and with my own eyes I saw some one jump into her car!—Could it, *could* it be possible that person was—*Ted?*"

Phyllis stared at her as if she thought Leslie certainly *had* "gone crazy." "There's not the slightest chance in the world!" she declared positively. "Why, only last night, when I was explaining to Ted about Eileen and how we'd become friends, all he said was: 'Well, so you've taken up with some other dame, have you! Might as well not have brought you down here, all the good you are to *us*, this time. Haven't been fishing with us more than twice since we came! Whoever this Eileen is, don't for goodness sake have her around here!' If he'd known her, he certainly would have shown it in some way. He acted utterly disgusted with me for having made her acquaintance!"

"That may all be true, but it doesn't prove that *he* is not acquainted with her," stubbornly affirmed Leslie.

And Phyllis was driven to acknowledge the force of the argument!

CHAPTER XIII

A TRAP IS SET

They went indoors at last and tried to settle down to reading, but it was very difficult to distract their minds from disturbing thoughts. Miss Marcia retired early, as the ride had tired her, and they were left to their own devices. At length they gave up the attempt to read and sat talking in whispers over the dying fire. When there was nothing left but ashes, Leslie suggested, with a shiver, that they go to bed, and they withdrew to Leslie's room.

Needless to say they did *not* go to bed at once, but sat long by the side window, staring across at Curlew's Nest. And it was then that Phyllis suddenly had her great idea.

"Now, see here, Leslie Crane, I have an idea and I'm going to do something, and I don't want you to interfere with me. Do you understand?"

"What do you mean?" whispered Leslie, looking alarmed.

"I mean just this. You're going to stay right where you are, with Rags, and keep watch. And I'm going to get out of the window and go over and explore Curlew's Nest by myself!"

"Phyllis, are you crazy?" implored Leslie. "I think that is one of the most dangerous things you could do!"

"Nothing of the sort. It's safer to-night than it would be almost any other time. Because—can't you see?—some one has evidently been here all the afternoon, when the coast was entirely clear, and no doubt they've done all they wish to do there for *this* day, anyhow! There couldn't *be* a better time than this very night, for there's not one chance in a hundred that they'll be back again."

"But just suppose the hundredth chance did happen, what would you do?" argued Leslie in despair.

"Do?—I'd shout like everything to you to turn Rags loose and call up the village constable and Father. Or better yet, I'd blow this police whistle which Father always insists on my carrying so that I can call them in to meals when they're down on the beach. If you hear *that*—just start things going. That's why I'm leaving you and Rags here on guard."

"Oh, I don't like it—I don't like it at all!" moaned Leslie. "It wouldn't be so bad if you only met Eileen there—but you can't tell whom you might encounter. I believe there's something more dangerous and desperate about this affair than either of us have guessed. I don't know why I think so—it's just come to me lately. It's a sort of—presentiment I can't seem to shake off!"

"Nonsense!" declared Phyllis, not to be balked. "If I met any one there, it could only be Eileen, and she's the one I'm crazy to encounter. After the way she has treated us, I'd have a few things to say to that young person for trespassing on Mrs. Danforth's property. Mrs. Danforth has always asked that we keep an eye on these cottages of hers while we're here,—it's an understood thing between us—so I'd be entirely within my rights in going in there to look the place over, especially if I suspected anything queer, and the other person would be quite in the wrong. Don't you see?"

"Oh, yes, I see that, but it doesn't lessen the fact that it may be dangerous!" sighed Leslie, wearily.

Phyllis ignored this. "If the hundredth chance should happen and I encounter Eileen, or if I come across anything very unusual and think you ought to see it, I'll let you know. Only in case of the hundred and *first* chance of real danger will I blow this whistle. Hold on tight to Rags and don't let him try to follow me. By-by! See you later!" And before Leslie could expostulate further, she had slipped out of the window, her electric torch in her hand, and was out of sight around the corner of the neighboring cottage.

Leslie remained half hanging out of the window, in an agony of suspense. The night was moonless and very dark. Added to that, a heavy sea-mist hung over everything like a blanket, and, out of the gloom, the steady pounding of the surf came to her with ominous insistence. The chill of the foggy air was penetrating, and she wrapped a sweater about her almost without realizing that she had done so. Rags was on the seat beside her, ears alertly cocked.

There was not a sound from the next house, nor could she even see a single gleam of light from the chinks in the shutters. Where could Phyllis be? Surely there had been time enough for her to have entered the place, looked about, and come out again. What could she be doing?

Then her brain began to be filled with horrible pictures of all the possible and impossible things that might have happened. So beyond all bearing did this feature become at length that she came to the sudden conclusion she would endure it no longer. She would get out of the window, herself, and go in search of her friend. If the worst came to worst, Rags could do some one a pretty bit of damage!

She had actually got as far as to put one foot over the low sill, when she quickly pulled it back again. A dark form had slipped around the corner of the other house and was hurrying toward her.

"Leslie! Leslie! Quick!—can you come here with me?"

Leslie almost collapsed, so swift was the reaction of relief at hearing Phyllis's voice, after all her terrible imaginings.

"What is it? What have you found?" she managed to reply.

"I can't explain to you here," whispered Phyllis. "It would take too long. Come along with me and see for yourself. It's perfectly safe. There's not a soul around. I've been in the house. Bring Rags along—it won't hurt. There have been queer doings here to-day—evidently. You can see it all in five minutes. Do come!"

In spite of all her previous fears, the temptation was too much for Leslie. If Phyllis had examined the ground and found it safe, surely there was no need for fear, and her curiosity to see what her friend had seen was now stronger than she could resist. She crept softly out of the window, speaking to Rags in a whisper, and the dog leaped lightly out after her.

They stole around the corner of the next house, three black shadows in the enveloping mist, and not till Phyllis had closed the side door of Curlew's Nest behind them was a word spoken.

"Follow me into the living-room," she ordered, "and if you don't see something there that surprises you, I miss my guess!"

She switched on the electric torch, and Leslie and Rags followed after her in solemn procession. From what she had said, Leslie expected to see the place in a terrible disorder, at the very least, and was considerably surprised, when she came into the room, to observe nothing out of its place. In some bewilderment she looked about, while Phyllis stood by, watching her.

"Why, what's wrong?" she whispered. "Everything seems to be just as it was."

"Look on the center-table!" commanded Phyllis, and she turned the torch full on that article of furniture.

Leslie tiptoed over to examine it. Then she uttered a little half-suppressed cry. On the table was a slip of paper—not a very large slip, and evidently torn from some larger sheet. And on this paper were a few words, type-written. She bent to read them. It ran:

It is advisable that the article stolen from its hiding-place be returned to it as speedily as possible, as otherwise, consequences most serious to all parties concerned will result.

Leslie turned deadly pale as she read it and seized Phyllis spasmodically by the arm.

"Oh, come out of here this moment!" she exclaimed. "I will not stay in this house another instant. I told you it was dangerous!" and she dragged her friend, with the strength of terror to the side door.

Outside, as the chill mist struck her, she breathed a great sigh of relief.

"What a little 'fraid-cat you are!" laughed Phyllis. "What in the world were you frightened about?"

Leslie shivered. "Oh, the whole thing strikes me as too uncanny for words! Some one has been in here and left that warning. They may be around here now, for all you know. Who do you suppose it can be?"

"I've a very good notion who it was, but it's too chilly to explain it standing here. Go over to the house with Rags and I'll be there directly. I want to go back a moment."

"Phyllis, Phyllis, *don't* go back there again!" implored Leslie, almost beside herself with an alarm she could hardly explain. "What do you want to do?"

"Never mind! Go back! I'll be there in two minutes." And tearing herself from Leslie's grasp, Phyllis ran back into the dark bungalow.

But Leslie would not return to her own house and desert her companion, though she could not bring herself to enter again that fear-inspiring place. So she lingered about outside in a state of unenviable desperation till Phyllis once more emerged from the dark doorway.

"So you couldn't leave me, after all!" Phyllis laughed. "Well, come back to bed now, and I'll tell you all about it."

They were chilled through with the drenching mist by the time they returned, and not till they were enveloped in the warm bed-clothing did Phyllis deign to explain her ideas about the newest development in their mystery.

"You were mightily scared by that little piece of paper, and I confess that I was startled myself, for a minute. But after I'd thought it over, it suddenly dawned on me that there was precious little to be scared about, and I'll tell you why. I'm perfectly convinced that that thing was written and placed there by my brother *Ted*!"

Leslie sat up in bed with a jerk. "You can't possibly mean it!"

"I certainly do, and here's my reason: You yourself convinced me, earlier this evening, that there was a chance of Ted's being mixed up in this thing somehow. I can't imagine how he got into it—that's a mystery past my explaining. But it looks very much as if he knew this Eileen, and that he was poking around here this afternoon while we were away. Now he suspects that *we* are mixed up in it, too, for he saw us come out of the bungalow that day. Well, if Eileen has told him about the Dragon's Secret and its disappearance, perhaps he thinks we know what happened to it. At any rate, he's taken the chance, and written this warning for our inspection the next time we happened in. He thinks it will scare us, I suppose! He'll presently find out that we don't scare for a cent! And I have thought of a scheme as good as his!— Do you know what I did when I went back there? I took a pencil and *printed* on the bottom of that paper just this:

"'*The article will be returned to its hiding-place.*'

"Now here's what I'm going to do next. In my trunk I have a little jewel-case, very much the size and shape and weight of the Dragon's Secret. It's one of those antimony things you've often seen, covered with a kind of carving that might easily pass for what's on that other one, if it weren't *seen*. I'm going to-morrow to make a burlap bag, just like the one we found, and sew the jewel-case in it, and it will be a sharp person who can tell the difference between them till the bag is opened. Then we'll bury it in the place where Rags dug up the other, some time to-morrow when the coast is clear. After that we'll wait and see what happens next! Now what do you think of my scheme?"

"It sounds splendid to me," admitted Leslie, then she added uneasily: "But there's something you haven't explained yet. You think Ted wrote that thing, yet it is *type-written*! How do you explain *that*?"

"Oh, that's simple enough! We have an old typewriter down here that Father uses occasionally, and Ted frequently practises on it."

"But did you notice the paper?" Leslie insisted. "It was queer, thin, almost foreign-looking stuff. Do you folks use that kind, or happen to have it about?"

"Oh, I don't know. I suppose he got it somewhere. What does it matter, anyway?" answered Phyllis, sleepily. And in two minutes more she was in the land of dreams.

But Leslie, still unconvinced, tossed the night through without closing her eyes.

CHAPTER XIV

THE MAN WITH THE LIMP

Two days had passed. To Leslie it was a constant marvel, considering the secret tension under which she lived, that outwardly her life went on in the same peaceful groove. She rose and dressed as usual, prepared the meals, ate and chatted with Aunt Marcia, walked on the beach or down to the village, fished occasionally with Phyllis and the Kelvins, took a dip in the ocean when it was not too chilly, read and slept and idled, as if there were nothing in the world but what was quiet and normal and in the ordinary course of things.

Aunt Marcia suspected nothing. Even Ted, who, she was certain, suspected many things, laughed and chatted with and teased her, and never by so much as a word or look indicated the slightest suspicion of her interest in Curlew's Nest and its affairs. With Phyllis his manner was somewhat different, and during the last two days their relations had seemed occasionally rather strained, but there was no open break, in public at least.

"But at home it's another matter!" Phyllis assured her. "Something's come over him—I can't guess what. He will hardly speak either to Father or myself. He doesn't even want to play his violin when we get together, and usually he adores that. He's moody and silent and just—*grouchy*, most of the time! And that's unusual for Ted. I'll give him credit for being a pretty amiable fellow, as a rule. I can't make him out!"

"And it surely is queer that we've seen nothing more of Eileen, don't you think so?" questioned Leslie.

"Well, no. Considering that she gained her point and got us away all that afternoon, I don't think it at all queer. She's done with us now. Why should she try to keep on with it? By the way, I called her up at Aunt Sally's last night. She wasn't there, but Aunt Sally said her grandfather has been rather worse for the last two days and she's been at the hospital most of the time—was there then. All of which may or may not be so. As a matter of fact, I guess Aunt Sally knows precious little of her doings when she's away in that car."

Somehow, Leslie could never believe Eileen quite as full of duplicity as Phyllis thought her. While she had to admit that circumstances made the girl's conduct seem almost inexcusable, there always lingered in her mind a stubborn feeling that perhaps there was more back of it all than they know—that Eileen herself might be struggling with entangling problems. And secretly she still felt a liking for the girl. But she knew it was useless to express these doubts to Phyllis, so she wisely kept her own counsel. But there was one thing she did allude to.

"Isn't it strange that Eileen never told us a word about her grandfather, or how sick he was, or what was the matter with him? You would have thought it natural, that day when she took us riding, to say *something* about it, anyway. I hardly see now how she could have avoided it. And yet she did. You'd never have thought she had such a thing as a sick grandfather on her mind!"

"Leslie, you certainly are a trusting soul!" exclaimed Phyllis, scornfully. "How do you know she *has* a sick grandfather in any hospital? I strongly doubt it myself!"

"Oh, I *can't* believe she's not telling the truth about *that!*" cried Leslie, thoroughly shocked. "Don't you believe anything about her any more?"

"I don't know what I believe or don't believe—about *her!*" retorted Phyllis. "And what's more, there's only one thing concerning her that I *am* interested in just now—whether she has discovered the answer to that note left in there and when she—or any one else—is going to make the attempt to unearth their treasure again!"

Phyllis had been as good as her word. On the morning after that night of the fog, she had returned to her bungalow before breakfast, and had reappeared later at Rest Haven with a mysterious bundle. When they had both retired to Leslie's room she revealed its contents, a piece of burlap, an exact duplicate of the one which contained the Dragon's Secret, and an antimony jewel-case. Then they got down the original from its dusty shelf, fashioned a bag, the exact size and shape of the one Rags had unearthed, placed the jewel-case in it, and sewed it up. When all was complete it would have been extremely difficult to tell the original from its duplicate, so nearly alike did they seem.

Late that afternoon, while Ted and his father were far up the inlet, and with the beach entirely deserted, they buried the false treasure-box in the sand by the old log. Phyllis did the deed, while Leslie scouted the beach in every direction, investigated every nook and corner that could possibly conceal any one, and made absolutely certain that they were not observed. And from that time on they had awaited results.

And to their certain knowledge, there had been none. Each day, at some hour when there was least likelihood of any one being near, they had examined the place, only to find the buried bag still in its hiding-place, untouched. At night they had taken turns keeping watch, all the night through; but no stealthy visitor had come to Curlew's

Nest, nor had there been any during the day—of that they were absolutely certain. The beach had never seemed so free of visitors before.

And thus matters stood on the second afternoon, and they were beginning to be impatient at inaction and delay. Then Phyllis had an idea.

"I know what's the matter!" she cried. "We're keeping too close a watch. We don't give anybody a chance to come within gunshot of that place, unobserved, so how can we expect that anything is going to happen? If it's Ted, don't you suppose he sees us hanging about here all the time? He'd be a goose to try anything right in front of our eyes. No doubt he's seen one or the other of us at the window all night, too. And if it's Eileen or any one else, it's the same thing. Let's go off somewhere and give them a chance. Not too far though, for we want to be where we can get back with reasonable speed ourselves."

So they went for a stroll along the beach, accompanied by Rags, who was only too delighted at the prospect of an expedition that promised some change. It was a mild, hazy October afternoon. An opalescent mist lay along the horizon and the waves rolled in lazily, too lazily to break with their accustomed crash. Every little while there would be a flight of wild geese, in V-shaped flying line, far overhead, and their honking would float down faintly as they pushed on in their southward course. It was a golden afternoon, and Leslie almost resented the fact that they had any worries or problems on their minds.

"Why, who in the world is that?" exclaimed Phyllis, suddenly, as they rounded a slight curve in the beach and came in sight of a figure standing at the water's edge, a rod and long line in his hand, and a camp-stool and fishing-kit beside him. "There hasn't been a stranger fishing in this region in an age! People generally go down by the big bungalow colony three miles farther along for that. We almost never see any one here. I wonder what it means!"

As they came nearer, they could see more plainly what sort of person he appeared to be. He was tall and stalwart and gray-haired. A slouch hat was pulled down to shade his eyes, but still they could see that his face was alert and kindly and placid, with twinkling gray eyes and a whimsical mouth. He was obviously an adept fisherman, as Phyllis remarked, when they had witnessed the clever way in which he managed a catch. They were very near him by that time, and watching breathlessly. Once his prey almost eluded him, but with a skilful manipulation of his tackle, he presently brought the big fellow, lashing wildly, to land, well out of reach of the water.

"Great Scott!" he exclaimed, winding up his line, "but that fellow gave me a warm ten minutes!"

The girls had by this time reached the spot and were admiring the catch.

"Congratulations!" laughed Phyllis, with the informal interest of the born fisherman. "I couldn't have done it myself, not after he had almost escaped. He must weigh five pounds!"

The stranger looked at them with interest. "So you fish? Well, it's the best sport in the world. This bouncer has been dodging me all the afternoon, and I vowed I'd get him before I left. Almost had him once before, but he got away with the bait. Wouldn't let me alone, though, even after that. I warned him he was flirting with his fate!" And he laughed a big, booming, pleasant laugh.

At this moment Rags, who had been elsewhere occupied, came bounding up, and straightway made a bee-line over to investigate the fish.

"Hi! Stop that!" exclaimed the stranger. "I intend to have that fish for my supper to-night!" and he made a dash for his cherished trophy. But Rags, disconcerted by the sudden movement, was on his guard at once. As the man approached, he sank his teeth into the fish with a growl that was a warning not to be ignored.

"Oh, call him off!" cried the man, anxiously, and Leslie, very much upset, sprang forward to rescue the stranger's dinner. But Rags saw a chance for a lark; and as times had been rather slow and uninteresting for him of late, he determined to make the most of it. Seizing the fish in a firm grip, he galloped madly up the beach, the two girls wildly pursuing.

There ensued a chase very similar to the one he had led them on that eventful day when he had unearthed the Dragon's Secret. Never once did he allow them to lay a finger on his prize, though, panting and disgusted, they pursued him hither and yon, sometimes so close that he was well within their reach, sometimes with him far in advance. Occasionally he would lie down with the fish between his paws, fairly inviting them to come and help themselves. Which they had no sooner attempted, than he was up and away again.

The man wisely took no part in the struggle, but stood looking on, encouraging them with half-rueful, half-laughing remarks. At length Leslie had an inspiration. While Rags was standing at the edge of the water, panting from a long and furious run, the fish reposing at his feet, she seized a small board lying near, called to him beguilingly and hurled the board out into the sea.

Here was a game that was even more fascinating. Rags always adored it. Forsaking the much-sought fish, he leaped into the lazy waves and swam out toward his new prize, while the stranger eagerly seized the fish and concealed it in his basket.

"Oh, I'm so sorry!" apologized Leslie. "I know he has spoiled it now. I hope you can forgive us for this dreadful thing."

"Nothing of the sort!" laughed the stranger. "He hasn't harmed it a bit, for it was only the head he had hold of. When it's washed and cooked, that beauty will taste just as good as if it had never had the adventure. My, but that's a fearsome animal of yours! I wouldn't want to tackle him. But those English sheep-dogs are noted for being wonderful protectors and very interesting pets besides."

And just to show that he bore Rags no malice, he picked up the board which the dog had retrieved, and obligingly hurled it into the surf again. Rags ecstatically pursued it once more, dropped it at the man's feet, and begged for another opportunity. But just before it was launched a third time, he spied a hermit-crab scuttling away almost under his nose, forsook his latest diversion, and was off on another hunt.

The man laughed, dropped the wet, sandy board, dusted off his hands by striking them together, picked up his fishing-kit, hung his camp-stool over his arm, bade the girls good afternoon, and strode away.

They gazed after him a moment and were about to turn back toward their own part of the beach, when Leslie suddenly seized Phyllis's arm in a vice-like grip.

"Phyllis, Phyllis, don't think me crazy! Something has just come to me. The way that man threw the board just now and dusted off his hands and then walked away—was just—exactly like—the *man with the limp* that morning at dawn! The action was identical. I'm positive I'm not mistaken. And he looks just like him, the same height and build and all, as he walked away."

"But, my dear child, *he doesn't limp!*" cried Phyllis, conclusively. "So you certainly are mistaken!"

"I know he doesn't, but I—don't care. He's the same one. I am absolutely sure of it. Maybe he's all over the limp now."

But though Leslie was so certain, Phyllis remained unconvinced!

CHAPTER XV
OUT OF THE HURRICANE

With the fickleness of October weather (which is often as freakish as that of April), the golden afternoon had turned cloudy and raw before the girls returned home. By nightfall it was raining, and a rising, gusty wind had ruffled the ocean into lumpy, foam-crested waves. At seven o'clock the wind had increased to a heavy gale and was steadily growing stronger. The threatened storm, as usual, filled Miss Marcia with nervous forebodings, and even Leslie experienced some uncomfortable apprehensions during their supper hour.

At eight o'clock, Phyllis arrived, escorted by Ted. "My!" she exclaimed, shaking the raindrops from her clothes as she stood on the porch, "but this is going to be a night! Father says the papers have warnings that we should probably get the tail-end of a West Indian hurricane that was headed this way, and I guess it has come! It's getting worse every minute. Have you seen how the tide is rising? Get on your things and come down to the beach. Ted brought me, because I could hardly stand up against the wind. He's going back presently. Come and see how the water is rising!"

"Oh, hush!" implored Leslie, glancing nervously toward her aunt. "You've no idea how upset Aunt Marcia is already," she whispered. "She'll be distracted if she gets an idea there's any danger."

"Forgive me!" returned Phyllis, contritely. "I really didn't think, for a moment. Father says there probably isn't any real danger. The tide has almost never risen as far as these bungalows, except in winter; and if the worst comes to the worst, we can always get out of them and walk away. But this threatens to be the worst storm of the kind we've had in years. Are you coming down to see the water?"

"If Aunt Marcia doesn't mind. But if she's afraid to be left alone, I won't."

"Oh, Ted will be here, and we'll just run down for a minute or two. It's really a great sight!"

Ted very thoughtfully offered to stay, and the two girls, wrapped to the eyes, pushed through the blinding rain and wind down to where the breakers were pounding their way up the beach, spreading, when they broke, farther and farther inland. So terrific was the impact of the wind, that the girls had to turn their backs to it when they wanted to speak.

"I brought you out here, as much as anything, because I had something to say," shouted Phyllis, her voice scarcely audible to the girl close beside her. "If the tide keeps on like this, it will probably wash away what we've hidden by the old log. And probably others who are concerned with that may be thinking of the same thing. We've got to keep a close watch. I believe things are going to happen to-night!"

"But don't you think we'd better dig it up ourselves, right away?" suggested Leslie. "We can't very well go out to do it later when it may be necessary, and surely you want to save it."

"Certainly *not*!" declared Phyllis. "I don't care if it *is* washed away. What I want is the fun of seeing the other parties breaking their necks to rescue it. If it's washed away they'll think the real article has disappeared, and then we'll see what next! Let's take one more look at the surf and then go back."

They peered out for a moment into the awe-inspiring blackness where an angry ocean was eating into the beach. Then, battling back against the wind, they returned to the house. Ted, having ascertained that there was no further service he could render, suggested that he had better go back and help his father stop a leak in the roof of Fisherman's Luck, which had suddenly proved unseaworthy.

"I'm so glad Phyllis will be with us to-night," Miss Marcia told him, "for I'm very little company for Leslie at a time like this. I get so nervous that I have to take a sedative the doctor has given me for emergencies, and that generally puts me pretty soundly to sleep."

They sat about the open fire after Ted had gone, listening to the commotion of the elements outside and talking fitfully. Every few moments Miss Marcia would rise, go to the window, and peer out nervously into the darkness. Once the telephone-bell rang and every one jumped. Leslie hurried to answer it.

"Oh, it's Aunt Sally Blake!" she exclaimed. "She wants to know how we all are and if we happen to have seen anything of Eileen. She was at the hospital all the afternoon, but she hasn't returned. Aunt Sally 'phoned the hospital, but they said Miss Ramsay had left three hours ago. She's terribly worried about her—thinks she may have had an accident in this storm. She thought it just possible Eileen might have come on out here. I said no, but would call her up later and see if she'd had news."

This latest turn of affairs added in no wise to Miss Marcia's peace of mind. "Why don't you take your powder now, Aunt Marcia, and go to bed," Leslie suggested at last. "It's only worrying you to sit up and watch this. There's no danger, and you might as well go peacefully to sleep and forget it. Phyllis and I will stay up quite a while yet, and if there's any reason for it, we will wake you."

Miss Marcia herself thought well of the plan and was soon in bed, and, having taken her sleeping-powder, the good lady was shortly fast and dreamlessly asleep, much to the relief of the girls.

"And now let's go into your room and watch," whispered Phyllis. "I'm just as certain as I can be that something is going to happen to-night!"

They arranged themselves, each at a window, Phyllis at the one toward the sea; Leslie facing Curlew's Nest, and began an exciting vigil. With the electric light switched off, it was so black, both inside and out, that it would have been difficult to distinguish anything, but with the windows shut and encrusted with wind-blown sand, it was utterly impossible. And when they dared to open them even a crack, the rain poured in and drenched them. They could do this only at intervals. Even Rags seemed to share the general uneasiness, and could find no comfortable spot in which to dispose himself, but kept hovering between the two windows continually.

It was Leslie who suddenly spoke in a hushed whisper. She had just opened her window the merest crack and peeped out, then closed it again without sound. "Phyllis, come here a moment. Look out when I open the window. It struck me that I saw something—some dark shape—slip around the corner of the house next door. See if you can see it."

Phyllis applied her eye to the crack when the window was opened. Then she drew her head back with a jerk. "I certainly did see something!" she whispered excitedly. "It slipped back to the other side of the bungalow!" She peered out again. "Good gracious! I see it again—or else it's another one. Doesn't seem quite like the first figure. Can there possibly be two?"

Leslie then, becoming impatient, demanded a turn at the peep-hole, and while she was straining her gaze into the darkness, they were both electrified by a light, timid knock at the door of the front veranda.

"Who can *that* be?" cried Leslie, wide-eyed and trembling.

"Perhaps it's Ted come back," ventured Phyllis. "At any rate, I suppose we'll have to go and see!"

Rags, alert also, uttered a low growl, and Leslie silenced him anxiously. "If this arouses Aunt Marcia,"—she whispered, "I shall be awfully worried. Be quiet, Rags!"

They tiptoed into the living-room, switched on the light, and advanced to the door. Again the knock came, light but insistent; and without further hesitation, Leslie threw the door open.

A muffled, dripping figure inquired timidly, "Please may I come in? I'm dripping wet and chilled to the bone."

"Why, *Eileen*!" cried Leslie, "what are you doing here in this terrible storm?"

"I got lost on the way back from the hospital," half sobbed the new-comer, "and I must have motored round and round in the rain and dark. And at last something went wrong with the engine, and I got out and left the car on the road—and I walked and walked—trying to find some place to stay—and at last I found I was right near here—so I came in!" She seemed exhausted and half hysterical and Leslie could not but believe her.

"Well, I'm so glad you're found and here!" she cried. "I must call up Aunt Sally right away and tell her you're all right. She called a while ago and was so anxious about you."

Leslie went to the telephone, while Phyllis helped Eileen to rid herself of her wet clothes and get into something dry. Then they all sat down by the fire in an uneasy silence. Presently Phyllis suggested that Eileen might like something warm to eat and drink, as she had evidently had no dinner. She assented to this eagerly, and the two girls went to the kitchen to provide something for her.

"I tell you," whispered Phyllis, "I just can't believe that hospital and getting-lost stuff! She came out here for some purpose, you mark my word! But why she wants to get in here is beyond me just yet. I'll find out later, though, you see if I don't!"

When they entered the living-room with a dainty tray a few minutes later, they found Eileen standing by one of the windows facing the ocean, trying vainly to peer into the outer blackness. She started guiltily when she saw them and retreated to the fire, murmuring something about "the awful night." But though she had seemed so eager for food, she ate almost nothing.

"Can't you take a little of this hot soup?" urged Leslie. "It will do you so much good. You must be very hungry by now."

"Oh, thanks, so much!" Eileen replied, with a grateful glance. "You are very good to me. I did really think I was hungry, at first, but I'm so nervous I just can't eat!"

She pushed the tray aside and began to roam restlessly about the room. At every decent excuse, such as an extra heavy gust of wind or a flapping of the shutters, she would hurry to the window and try to peer out.

At length Phyllis made an excuse to disappear into Leslie's room and was gone quite a time. Suddenly she put her head out of the door into the living-room and remarked, in a voice full of suppressed excitement: "Leslie, can you come here a moment?"

Leslie excused herself and ran to join Phyllis. "What is it?" she whispered breathlessly.

"Look out of the front window!" returned Phyllis, in a hushed undertone. "There's something queer going on outside—by the old log!"

Leslie opened the window a crack. The howl of the storm and the lash of rain was appalling, and it was two or three minutes before she could accustom her sight to the outer blackness. But when she did manage to distinguish something, she was startled to observe not only one, but *two* dark figures circling slowly round and round the log, like two animals after the same prey, and watching each other cautiously.

"But that's not all!" muttered Phyllis, behind her. "There's a third figure standing in the shadow right by Curlew's Nest. I saw him out of the side window. What on earth can it all mean?"

So absorbed were they that neither of them noticed the form that slipped into the room behind them and stood peering over their shoulders. But they were suddenly startled beyond words to hear Eileen, close behind them, catch her breath with an indrawn hiss, and mutter involuntarily:

"Oh, *Ted!*—Be careful!—Look out!—*Look out!—*"

CHAPTER XVI

RAGS TO THE RESCUE

Phyllis whirled about. "What is the matter? Why do you say that?" she demanded in a fierce whisper.

Eileen shrank back, evidently appalled by what she had unconsciously revealed. "I—I—didn't mean anything!" she stammered.

"You certainly did!" Phyllis declared. "You said something about 'Ted.' Who *is* 'Ted,' and what is going on outside there?"

"Oh, I don't know!—I'm not—sure! I'm dreadfully nervous—that's all."

"Look here!" cried Phyllis, with stern determination, "I believe you know a great deal more than you will acknowledge. You've said something about 'Ted.' Now, I have a brother Ted, and I've reason to think he has been mixed up with some of your affairs. I wish you would kindly explain it all. I think there's some trouble—out there!"

"Oh, I can't—I oughtn't," Eileen moaned; when suddenly Leslie, who had glanced again out of the window, uttered a half-suppressed cry:

"Oh, there *is* something wrong! They're—they're struggling together—for something!"

Both of the other girls rushed to the window and peered out over her shoulder. There was indeed something decidedly exciting going on. The two figures who had been circling about the old log, watching each other like a couple of wild animals, were now wrestling together in a fierce encounter. How it had come about, the girls did not know, as none of them had been looking out when it began. But it was plainly a struggle for the possession of something that one of them had clutched tightly in his hand. Vaguely they could see it, dangling about, as the contest went on. And each, in her secret heart, knew it to be the burlap bag—and its contents!

"Eileen!" cried Phyllis, turning sharply upon the other girl, "is one of those two—my brother Ted? Answer me—truthfully."

"Yes—oh, yes!" panted Eileen.

"And is he in—danger?" persisted Phyllis.

"Oh—I'm afraid so!"

"Then I'm going out to help him!" declared Phyllis, courageously. "Come, Leslie—and bring Rags!"

Leslie never afterward knew how it happened—that she, a naturally timid person, should have walked out of that house, unhesitatingly and unquestioningly, to do battle with some unknown enemy in the storm and the dark. If she had had any time to think about it, she might have faltered. But Phyllis gave her no time. With Rags at their heels, they snatched up some wraps and all suddenly burst out of the front door onto the veranda, Phyllis having stopped only long enough to take up her electric torch from the living-room table. She switched this on in the darkness, and, guided by its light, they plunged into the storm.

The force of the wind almost took their breath away. And as they plowed along, Leslie was horrified to notice that the tide had crept almost up to the level of the old log and was within sixty feet of the bungalow. "Oh, what *shall* we do if it comes much higher!" she moaned to herself. But from that moment on, she had little time for such considerations.

Phyllis had plunged ahead with the light, and the two other girls followed her in the shadow. Leslie was somewhat hampered in her advance, as she was holding Rags by his collar and he strongly objected to the restraint. But she dared not let him loose just then.

Suddenly they were plunged in utter darkness. Phyllis's torch had given out! And the two others, reaching her side at that instant, heard her gasp, "Oh, dreadful! Can anything be the matter with this battery?" But after a moment's manipulation the light flashed on again. It was in this instant that they saw the face of Ted, lying on the ground and staring up at them while his assailant held him firmly pinned beneath him in an iron grip.

"Help!" shrieked Ted, above the roar of the wind. "Let Rags loose!"

They needed no other signal. Leslie released her hold on the impatient animal, and with a snarl that was almost unnerving, he darted, straight as an arrow, for Ted's assailant.

The girls never knew the whole history of that encounter. They only realized that Ted finally emerged from a whirling medley of legs and arms, limping but triumphant, and strove to loosen the dog's grip on a man who was begging to be released.

"That'll do, Rags, old boy! You've done the trick! Good old fellow! Now you can let go!" he shouted at the dog, trying to persuade him to loosen his hold. But Rags was obdurate. He could see no point in giving up the struggle at this interesting juncture.

"Call him off!" Ted shouted to the girls, "I can't make him let go!"

"Is it *safe?*" cried Phyllis, in answer.

"We'll have to take a chance!" he answered. "He's half killing this fellow!"

With beating heart Leslie came into the range of the light, grasped Rags by the collar and pulled at him with all her might. "Come Rags! Let go! It's all right!"

The dog gave way reluctantly. And when he had at length loosed his terrible grip and was safely in Leslie's custody, the man scrambled to his feet, rose, held on to his arm with his other hand, and groaned.

And, despite his disheveled condition and his drenched appearance, in the glare of the electric torch the girls recognized him, with a start of amazement. It was the fisherman of the afternoon—the man with the former limp!

In the glare of the electric torch the girls recognized him

He turned immediately on Ted with an angry, impatient gesture. "Well, the other fellow got it—after all! I don't know what business *you* had in this concern, but you spoiled the trick for me—and didn't do yourself any good! And if that dog gives me hydrophobia, I'll sue the whole outfit of you! He beat it off in that direction—the other fellow. I saw that much. I can't lose any time, though what I need is a doctor."

And with another angry snort, he disappeared into the darkness and the hurricane.

CHAPTER XVII

EILEEN EXPLAINS

It was an amazed, bewildered, and sheepish group that faced each other in the light of the electric torch after the departure of the unknown man. Phyllis was the first to recover self-possession.

"Well, we might as well go indoors," she remarked, in her decided way. "There's evidently nothing to be gained by staying out here in the storm!"

The others, still too benumbed in mind to have any initiative of their own, followed her obediently. Only when they were at the door did Leslie arouse to the immediate urgencies.

"Do please be very quiet and not wake Aunt Marcia!" she begged. "I'm afraid the effect on her would be very bad if she were to realize all that has happened here."

They entered the bungalow on tiptoe, removed their drenched wraps, and sank down in the nearest chairs by the dying fire.

"And now," remarked Phyllis, constituting herself spokesman, as she threw on a fresh log and some smaller sticks, "we'd be awfully obliged to you, Ted and Eileen, if you'll kindly explain what this mystery is all about!"

"I don't see why under the sun *you* had to come butting into it!" muttered Ted, resentfully, nursing some bruises he had sustained in the recent fray.

"Please remember," retorted Phyllis, "that if I hadn't come butting into it—and Leslie and Rags,—you'd probably be very much the worse for wear at this moment!"

"That's so! Forgive me, old girl! You *did* do a fine piece of work—all of you. I'm just sore because the thing turned out so—badly. But what I really meant was that I can't see how you got mixed up in it at all—from the very beginning, I mean."

"That's precisely what we think about *you*!" laughed Phyllis. "We've felt all along as if it were *our* affair and that *you* were interfering. So I think we'd better have explanations all around!"

"Well, as a matter of fact, it's Eileen's affair, most of all, so I think she'd better do her explaining first," Ted offered as a solution of the tangle.

They all looked toward Eileen, sitting cowered over the fire, and she answered their look with a startled gaze of her own.

"I—I don't know whether I ought!" she faltered, turning to Ted. "Do you think I ought?"

"I guess you'd better!" he declared. "It's got to a point where these folks seem to have some inside information of their own that perhaps might be valuable to you. How they got it, I can't think. At any rate, there'll be no harm done by it, I can vouch for that. So—just fire away!"

Thus adjured, Eileen drew a long breath and said hesitantly:

"I—I really don't know just where to begin. A lot of it is just as much a mystery to me as it is to you. I think you all have heard that I have a grandfather who is very ill, in a hospital over in Branchville. He is the Honorable Arthur Ramsay, of Norwich, England. He has been for many years a traveler and explorer in China and India and Tibet. Early this year he had a severe attack of Indian fever and could not seem to recuperate, so he started for England, coming by way of the Pacific and America. When he got to the Atlantic coast, this last summer, some one recommended that he should try staying a few weeks at this beach; so he took a bungalow and spent part of the summer and autumn here, and thought he was much benefited."

"Do excuse me for interrupting!" exclaimed Phyllis; "but was the bungalow he rented Curlew's Nest?"

"Why, yes," hesitated Eileen, with a startled glance at her "it—it was."

"Then, do you mind telling me how it was that the name was so different?" persisted Phyllis. "Mrs. Danforth understood that she rented it to a Mr. Horatio Gaines."

"Oh, that was because Grandfather didn't want it in his own name, because, you see, he's a rather well-known person in England and even over here, and he needed a complete rest, with no danger of having to be interviewed or called upon or anything like that. So he had his man, Geoffrey Horatio Gaines, hire the place, and transact all the business here in *his* name. It saved Grandfather a lot of trouble, for Geoffrey simply took charge of everything; and as Grandfather never went among people here, no one was the wiser.

"After he left the cottage, he expected to go to New York and remain there till he sailed for home. And he *did* go there for a few days, but his health at once grew worse, so he returned to the beach. Of course, the bungalow was closed by that time, so he took rooms at the hotel, farther along. It was there that I joined him. I had come over here with friends of Mother's, earlier in the summer, and had been visiting at their summer camp in the Adirondacks until I should join Grandfather and return to England with him.

"I hadn't been with him more than two or three days when I realized that something had gone awfully wrong, somehow or other. Grandfather was worried and upset about something, and he began to watch his mail and be anxious to avoid meeting any one. He couldn't or wouldn't explain things to me, but had long interviews with his man, Geoffrey, who has been with him for years and years and whom he trusts completely.

"At last, one awfully stormy night, about two weeks ago, Geoffrey disappeared, and has never been seen or heard of since. We can't imagine what has become of him. And the next day Grandfather was so worried about him and the other troubles that a cold he had ran into a severe attack of pneumonia. Of course, it wasn't feasible for him to remain at the hotel, especially as it was soon to close, so he had himself taken to the nearest good hospital, which happened to be this one at Branchville. Since he didn't have Geoffrey to wait on him, he wanted to be where he could have the best attention and nursing, and as I could run his car, which Geoffrey had always done, I could get easily there to see him. Then, as you probably know, the hotel closed for the season, and the manager very kindly found me a place to stay—with Aunt Sally Blake—in the village. She has been very good and kind to me, but I expect I've worried her a lot, not because I didn't care, but because I couldn't help it and I couldn't tell her about—things!

"But, oh! I have been so troubled—so fairly *desperate*, at times! You cannot even guess the awful burden I've had to bear—and all alone,—at least till I came quite by accident to know your brother Ted. He has helped me so much—but that is another part of the story!

"One night Grandfather's fever was very high and he was delirious. I begged his nurse to let me sit with him awhile, and I heard him constantly muttering about the bungalow, and Geoffrey hiding something there, and it being safe at Curlew's Nest, and a lot more half-incoherent remarks of that kind. Next morning he was a little better and in his right mind again, so I asked him what he had meant by the things he had talked about the night before. And then he said:

"'Eileen, I'll have to trust you with some of the secret, I believe, since you've overheard what you have. Perhaps you may even be able to help, and of course I can trust you to keep your own counsel—absolutely. There's been a very mysterious mix-up here, and it involves far more than you may imagine. In fact, it might even become an affair of international moment—if something is not found, and quickly too. The gist of the matter is this: while I was in China last year, I had some informal correspondence with an official very high in government circles there, concerning his attitude in regard to the province of Shantung. As he was inclined to be very friendly toward me at the time he was just a little expansive and indiscreet (I think those were Grandfather's words) in regard to his Government's plans. Later, I think, he regretted this, and made some half-joking overtures to have his letters returned. But I pretended not to understand him and the matter was dropped. As a matter of fact, I thought them too suggestive and important to my own Government to part with them!'

"It is these letters that are the heart of the whole trouble, Grandfather says. He heard nothing more about them till he came to stay at the hotel here. Then he received a very threatening letter, declaring that if this packet was not returned to the writer, serious consequences would result. It didn't say *what* consequences, but Grandfather suspected they might even go as far as an attempt on his life. But he was determined not to give up the letters. You see, they concerned a matter that might involve his own country with China, and he felt they should be delivered to his own Government. Beside that, he is just stubborn enough not to be bullied into anything by threats.

"His man Geoffrey tried to persuade him to put the letters in a safe-deposit vault in New York, but Grandfather says he is old-fashioned in some things and doesn't trust even to safe-deposit boxes—says he prefers to keep things he values in his own possession. He had the letters in a queer little bronze box that was given him, years ago, by the late Empress Dowager of China. It had a secret lock that was quite impossible to open unless one knew the trick. He carried this in his pocket, and slept with it under his pillow at night, and felt perfectly safe about it."

Here Eileen paused a moment for breath, and the two other girls glanced at each other guiltily, but they said nothing. Then Eileen went on:

"One night, just after I came, there was an attempt to rob him at the hotel. The attempt failed because Geoffrey happened to be awake and discovered some one prowling about Grandfather's sitting-room. Whoever it was escaped through the window without even his face being seen, and there was no trace of him later. Grandfather made Geoffrey keep the thing quiet and not report it to the hotel, because he didn't want any publicity about the matter. But he decided then that it would be safer to have the thing hidden somewhere for a time—in some place where no one would dream of hunting for it. And it struck him that down at the bungalow where he had spent those quiet weeks, and which he supposed was all shut up and deserted, would be as unlikely a spot as any to be suspected of hiding such a thing. He supposed that the one next door—this one—was closed also, or I do not think he would have considered that hiding-place.

"So the next night, which happened to be one when there was a very hard storm, he sent Geoffrey down to the bungalow with the little box containing the letters. He did not wish him to take the car, as it might be too conspicuous, but had him go on foot. Geoffrey had found out, during the summer, that one could get into that place through a door at the side by working at the hook through the crack with a knife-blade, and he intended to get into the cottage and conceal the box in some out-of-the-way hiding-place there.

"But here is where the mystery begins. Geoffrey set off that night, but has never been seen or heard of since. What has happened to him, we cannot imagine, unless he was caught and taken a prisoner by some one concerned in getting those letters. If he had been killed, we would surely know it. Yet if he were alive, it seems as if we should have heard from him, somehow. He was a most devoted and faithful and trustworthy soul, so we are sure that something must have happened to him—that he is being detained somewhere. Grandfather is quite certain that he is guarding the secret of that box, somehow, and that it would be best to wait till he comes back or sends us some word.

"What Grandfather asked me to do was to run out here in the car some day, and, if there was no one about, to scout around and see if I could discover any clue to the mystery, without attracting attention. He supposed, of course, that the beach was by that time entirely deserted. I came out the very next day, but found to my disgust that the cottage next door was occupied—by you, as I now know! But I felt it would not be wise to be seen about here in the daytime, so, without saying anything to Grandfather (who would be awfully upset if he knew it), I determined to run out about ten o'clock that night and scout around when you people would probably be in bed.

"And here is where Ted comes into it! I got here that night as I had planned, found no one about, and tried the experiment of getting into the side door, as Grandfather had explained, but I found it very difficult; in fact, quite impossible—for *me!* And while I was fussing with it, I was suddenly startled by a low voice, right behind me, inquiring *very* politely what I was trying to do! It was Ted, here, who had been out for a stroll, and happening to catch a glimpse of me at this very peculiar occupation, and naturally thinking I was a burglar, had come up unobserved to find out about it!

"You can just imagine what an *awful* position it was for me! I did not know what to say or what to do. I know that, legally, I had no business there, and if he were inclined to make a fuss about it, he could have me arrested. I literally almost went out of my mind at that moment. But I guess something must have made him feel that I wasn't really a 'lady burglar' or anything of that sort, for he just said, very kindly, 'If you are in trouble, perhaps I can help you!'

"I didn't see how he could possibly help me unless he knew the whole story, and I thought I ought not tell any one *that!* But unless I did, I was certainly in a very terrible position. So I suddenly made up my mind it would have to be done, for something made me feel he was honorable and trustworthy, and that the secret would be safe with him. What made me feel all the more sure was that he mentioned that he was staying up the beach at his father's bungalow, and had happened to be out for a walk and had seen me there. I know he said it to make me feel easier, and that everything was all right.

"So I told him as much as I could of the story. And when he had heard it, he said: 'I happen to know all about opening that door, because I know the people who own the cottage very well. Perhaps you had better let me try.' I said I'd be only too glad to, and he had the door unfastened in a moment. Then he told me to go in and examine the place all I wished to and he would watch outside. If I needed any help, I could call and he would come in and do what he could for me.

"Well, I went in and examined the whole place with my electric torch, but I could not discover a single thing except that one of the bricks in the fireplace had been partly loosened and a broken knife-blade was in the corner of the chimney-place. It was the only thing I could see to show that possibly Geoffrey had been there. I thought the knife-blade looked like one I had seen him use.

"But as I didn't see a sign of the bronze box, I knew it was useless to stay any longer, so I came out. Ted fastened the door again, went with me to the car, which I had left down the road, and offered to give me any further help he could, at any time. He promised to keep the secret from every one, and said that he would make an even more thorough search over Curlew's Nest, if I wished, because he had much better opportunity to do so. Of course, I agreed to that and went on back to Aunt Sally's.

"Two days later, Ted saw my car going along one of the back roads near the village, signaled to me, and told me that, the day before, he had caught you girls coming out of Curlew's Nest and that you acted rather guilty and refused to explain what you had been in there for. He told me that you might possibly suspect something, and to steer clear of you if we should happen to encounter each other, as it is always likely that people will, in this town. He described what you both looked like, so that I couldn't fail to know you.

"And, sure enough, I met you both that very morning, in Mrs. Selby's little store, and I expect you think I acted in a perfectly abominable manner. I just hated to do it, for I liked the looks of you both, but I felt I must take no chances. Ted also told me that he had been in Curlew's Nest the night before and had gone over the place very carefully once more, but had found nothing except a string of beads that had been torn from the fringe of my girdle that other night, and had been lying on the floor. I remember that the girdle caught when I was looking under one of the bureaus. He also gave me the broken penknife-blade to keep, as he said it was best to leave nothing around there that any one else could discover and use as a clue.

"A day or two later I met you, Phyllis, at Aunt Sally's and she *would* insist on introducing us, though I could see you were no more anxious to make the acquaintance, after the way I'd acted, than I was. But I encountered Ted again that afternoon, and he said he had hunted me up to tell me he had news and also a plan that he wanted to suggest. He said he had noticed, during the last two or three days, a strange man who seemed to haunt the beach, just a short way off and out of sight of the two bungalows. The man seemed to be a very ardent fisherman,—and an expert one, too,—but Ted had noticed that he kept a very sharp lookout toward the bungalows when he thought no one was around to see. He suspected that perhaps this man had something to do with the mystery.

"The plan he suggested was that I get acquainted with you girls, after all, in some way that seemed the most natural, but without letting you know that I was also acquainted with *him*. And when I had done so, I had better offer to take you all out for a long drive in the car and keep you away a good while, and give him a chance to see what this man was up to—if anything.

"The getting acquainted was easy, and you all know how I managed *that*—and also the ride, a day or two later. When I was returning from the ride that night, at dusk, Ted signaled me from the bushes near Curlew's Nest, jumped into the car, and told me what had happened in the afternoon. He had gone off to the village first, then hurried back, slipped up here by way of the creek, and hidden himself in a clump of rushes across the road. Just as he had suspected, he saw his suspicious fisherman sneak up here after a while, scout around the outside of the bungalow, disappear into it for a time, by the side door, come out, apparently empty-handed, stare at the outside again for a long time, and then at your bungalow, and finally disappear. But that was not all.

"He waited where he was a few minutes, thinking possibly the man might come back, and he was just about to come out, when along came an automobile with *two* men in it, which stopped directly in front of Curlew's Nest. He could not see their faces, for they had slouch hats pulled far down on their heads. They got out and walked about a bit, evidently to see if any one was around. Then, thinking themselves alone, they hurried up to the bungalow, worked at the side door, and finally got in. Shortly after, they came out again and walked down to the beach, where he could not see them. Then they came back, got into the car, and drove off.

"By that time it was growing so late that he concluded he would stay where he was and wait for me to come back, which he did. Before he left me, we had a slight breakdown, and in helping me fix it, he hurt his hand. But that same night, long after midnight, he got into Curlew's Nest again to see if he could find out what had happened, and he found a very strange message left on the table—a type-written warning to the one who had taken the article (as it was called!) from its hiding-place to return it, and underneath, a printed note in pencil, saying it would be returned. He thought probably the first man had left the type-written part, and the other two had printed the answer underneath. That was all he could make of it.

"It was all very mysterious, but while we couldn't make much out of it, at least it showed that something concerning the affair was going on and that the place must be closely watched. Ted volunteered to keep this watch. Meanwhile, Grandfather had had a very bad turn and I was with him constantly. He was terribly depressed over the whole affair. Even his doctor, who knows nothing about this, said he was evidently worrying about something, and if the cause of worry were not removed, he doubted the possibility of recovery. Tonight I stayed with him later than usual, and in returning, actually did lose my way in the storm. But when I at last discovered where I was, I knew that it was not far from here and could not resist the temptation to come over and see if anything was happening. I found Ted also scouting around, and suddenly we realized that some one else was on the ground too, though we could not tell *who*, in the darkness and rain. But Ted thought it very dangerous for me to be out there, so he made me come in here, as I did. And I need not tell you what happened after that!"

Eileen ceased speaking, and Phyllis had just opened her lips to say something when there was a knock at the door. All four jumped nervously, but Ted got up and went to open it.

To their immense alarm, the opened door revealed the figure of—"the man with the limp!"

CHAPTER XVIII

THE DRAGON GIVES UP THE SECRET

THE man also started back at the sight of all four of them together. And Rags, who had been drying himself quietly by the fire, rose with a snarl and leaped toward his enemy of the earlier part of the evening.

"Heavens! don't let that animal loose on me again!" cried the man, backing off. "I've just been down to the village doctor and had my arm cauterized, as it is. I stopped in to tell you something you'd better know. Probably you haven't noticed it, if you haven't looked out recently. The water is rising rapidly and will soon be very nearly up to your bungalow. You may want to get out before it sweeps under it!"

With a cry of alarm, they all leaped toward the door, Ted grasping Rags firmly by the collar. It was even as the man had said. Peering through the darkness, they could see the water spreading inward from a recent breaker, only about twenty-five feet from the veranda. And the next breaker spread in even a few inches further.

"What *shall* we do?" cried Leslie. "Aunt Marcia will be frightened to death if she knows it, and how I'm to get her out of here in this howling storm, or where I can take her, I can't imagine!"

But Ted had been critically examining the weather. "Don't worry, Leslie!" he soothed her. "The wind is shifting. I noticed just now that it seemed to be around to the north and is getting farther west also. That means the storm is almost over. And the tide ought to turn in ten minutes or so. It's practically at its highest now. Ten chances to one it won't rise more than a foot or two further. But we'll keep watch, and if it does, we'll get your aunt out of here in Eileen's car, which is just down the road, and take her either to our place or to the village. Our bungalow isn't likely to be damaged, as it's farther up the dune than these. Don't worry!"

Thus encouraged, Leslie turned indoors again, and the man, who was still lingering on the porch, remarked:

"If it isn't too much trouble, friends, I'd like to come in for a minute or two and ask you folks a few questions about that little fracas this evening and how you came to be mixed up in it. It's all right and perfectly proper!" he hastened to add, seeing their startled glances. "I can show you my credentials." He opened his coat and exhibited a shield on his vest—the shield of a detective of the New York police force!

So amazed were they that they could scarcely reply, but the man took matters in his own hands and walked into the house. And Leslie never even thought to warn him to speak softly because of Aunt Marcia!

Unconsciously they grouped themselves about him at the open fire. And Rags, now that the obnoxious stranger had been admitted to the house on a hospitable footing, made no further demonstrations of enmity.

"My name is Barnes—Detective Barnes of the New York force," he began, "and I'd like to clear up one or two little puzzles here before I go on with this business. It's a rather peculiar one. I heard this young gentleman refer to a car that was standing in the road near here and say it belonged to one of you young ladies named Eileen. I'd like to inform Miss Eileen that the party who got that little article we were all scrapping for to-night, jumped into her car when he got to the road, tore like mad in it to the station, left it there, and caught the express for New York. I was just in time to see him disappearing in it, but of course *I* had to walk to the village. I suspected what he was going to do, though, and I went straight to the station and found the car standing there. So I took the liberty of getting in it, driving myself to the village doctor, and then back out here. You will find your car, Miss Eileen, standing just where you left it, but I thought you'd like to know it had had the little adventure!"

Eileen opened her mouth to reply, but the man gave her no chance, turning immediately to Ted. "And as for you, young man, I suppose you thought you were doing a wonderful stunt when you landed into me to-night, just as I'd unearthed the thing I've been on the trail of for a week; but I'll have to tell you that you've spoiled one of the prettiest little pieces of detective work I've undertaken for several years, and may have helped to precipitate a bit of international trouble, beside. I don't know what your motive was,—I suppose you thought me a burglar,—but—

"Just a moment!" cried Eileen, springing forward. "Tell me, why are you concerned in this? My name is Ramsay and I have a right to ask!"

Detective Barnes was visibly startled. "Are you a relative of the Honorable Arthur Ramsay?" he demanded; and when she had told him, he exclaimed: "Then you must know all about Geoffrey Gaines and how he disappeared!"

"I've known him since I was a baby," she answered; "but how he disappeared is still an awful mystery to us. My grandfather is very ill in the Branchville hospital, you know."

"But didn't he receive my letter?" cried Mr. Barnes. "I sent it two days ago!"

"He has been too ill to read any mail for the last two days," replied Eileen, "and, of course, I have not opened it."

"Well, that explains why I haven't heard from him!" the man exclaimed, with a sigh of relief. "Then I guess you will be interested to hear that Gaines is alive and well, but kept a close prisoner by some heathen Chinese in a house on a west side street in New York."

"But how?—Why?—Did it happen the—the night he—came down here?" she ventured.

"I see you're pretty well informed about the matter," he remarked cautiously. "And if these others are equally so, I guess it's safe for me to go on and give you a history of the thing."

Eileen nodded, and he went on:

"Gaines and I used to know each other in England, years before he entered your grandfather's service. In fact, we had been schoolmates together. Then I came over to this country and entered the detective service, and he went into another walk of life. But we kept in touch with each other by writing occasionally. A week or so ago I was astonished to receive a letter from him, written on all sorts of odds and ends of paper and in an envelope plainly manufactured by himself. It contained some very singular news.

"It gave me first the history of those letters and how anxious your grandfather was to keep hold of them. Then it told how he (Gaines) had taken the box down here that night and tried first to conceal it in the bungalow. But no place in the house seemed safe enough to him. He tried to dig up a brick in the fireplace and bury it there, but gave it up after he had broken his knife in the attempt. Then he had the inspiration to bury it in the sand somewhere outside, and he described where he *did* locate it, right by that log. If Gaines had known much about the tides here, he wouldn't have thought that a very good scheme. He didn't, though, and thought he'd found an excellent place. He then turned to walk back to the hotel, but hadn't gone more than a mile (it was storming hard, if you remember) when a terrific blow on the back of the head knocked him senseless. He never knew another thing until he came to, after what must have been a number of days, to find himself a prisoner in a house he judged to be somewhere in New York. And from his description I've located it about west Sixty-first street.

"He appeared to be in the keeping of a Chinaman who dressed American fashion and spoke good English. He was told that he was a prisoner and that it was hopeless to try to communicate with any one until he had reported exactly where and how those letters had been concealed. He begged for a day or two to consider the matter and was granted it, but told that if he did not comply with their wishes he would disappear for good and no one would ever be the wiser.

"In the meantime, he managed to get together a few scraps of paper, and with the stub of a pencil he happened to have about him, he wrote this letter to me, describing the location of the letters and how he had hidden them in a bronze box wrapped in a burlap bag. He urged me to go and get them at once, and then, later, he could safely describe to his captors where he had hidden them. Perhaps you wonder how he expected to get this letter to me, since he was so carefully guarded. He said that he was on the third floor, front, of the house, near a corner where he could see a post-box. He happened to have a solitary stamp in his pocket, which he put on the letter. Then, at some hour when he thought his captors were busy elsewhere, he expected to attract the attention of some children playing in the street and offer to throw them some money if they would mail the letter in the nearby box. As I received the letter, no doubt his plan worked successfully. At any rate, I got it a week ago and started on the trail immediately.

"I landed out here one morning while it was still dark, and dug all around the spot mentioned, but couldn't find a trace of the bag or box."

"Oh, I saw you that morning!" cried Leslie. "But when you walked away you seemed to stoop and had a bad limp! I don't understand!"

"I know you saw me," he smiled, "or, at least, that *some* one did, for as I happened to glance back at this house, it was growing just light enough for me to realize there was some one watching at the window. So I adopted that stoop and limp as I walked away, just so you would not be likely to recognize me if you saw me again. It is a ruse I've often practised."

"But it didn't work *that* time," laughed Leslie, "for I recognized you again this afternoon by the way you dusted the sand off your hands and threw away the stick!"

"Well, you are certainly a more observing person than most people!" he answered gravely. "But to go on. Of course, I was very much disappointed, but I remained here, staying at the village hotel, and kept as close a watch on the place as was possible, pretending all the time that I was here on a fishing excursion. I tried very hard to keep out of sight of these bungalows, in the daytime, anyway. The day you all went off on the auto ride the coast seemed clear, and I went through the place. But I hadn't been out of it long and walked down to the beach, when I saw the two men drive up in a car and enter the bungalow also, and later come out to dig by that old log. Of course, they didn't see me about! I took care of that. And I knew, beyond a doubt, that they were Gaines's Chinamen, come to find the booty.

"Of course they didn't find it, any more than I had, and I felt sure they would go back and make it hot for Gaines, and I judged that he would probably try to gain time in some way. I went back to my hotel that night to think it all over and make further plans, and didn't visit the bungalow again till next evening, when I found to my astonishment a queer note, type-written, on the table there—a warning that the article stolen from its hiding-place had better be returned. And under it, a reply, printed in lead-pencil, saying it would be returned."

"I couldn't make head or tail of the business. I judged the type-written part to have been left by the Chinese. But who had scribbled the other was a dark-brown mystery. At any rate, I concluded that to-night would probably be the crucial time, and determined to get in ahead of every one else. The storm was a piece of good fortune to me, as it concealed things so well, and about nine o'clock I was on the spot, proceeding to dig down by the old log. Pretty soon I realized, though, that there was some one else around. And just as I'd unearthed the bag, which *had* been mysteriously returned to its hiding-place, you appeared out of somewhere, young man, fell on me like a thousand of bricks, and we had a grand old tussle. I'll give you credit for being *some* wrestler, but I was getting the best of it, when along came you others with that terrible beast and did the business for me!

"I thought all along, though, that you, Mr. Ted, were one of the Chinamen. But that person must have been on the scene also, probably lurking in the shelter of the bungalow and watching the fracas. And when your electric light blazed on the scene, Miss," he turned to Phyllis, "he no doubt saw the bag in my hand. Then, when the light went out for a moment, he rushed in and grabbed the prize and was off while we two were so busy with one another!

"It was a losing game all around. While I was in the village, I 'phoned my department in New York to meet his train when it got in and arrest him, if they could find him, and search him at once. But after I'd been to the doctor's (I had a long session there) I 'phoned them again and heard that the train had been met, but no one answering such description as I could give had got off. No doubt he was canny enough to get off at some station short of New York and so was lost to sight.

"Well, the prize is lost for this time, but perhaps we can pick up the trail again. At any rate, Gaines is probably free, for they promised to release him as soon as the letters were obtained."

When he had ceased speaking, Leslie got up from her chair and disappeared into the kitchen. When she returned, she laid a dark bundle in the lap of Eileen.

"I guess the prize was found some time ago!" she remarked quietly. "Suppose you open that bag and see, Eileen!"

And amid an astounded silence, Eileen's fingers managed to unloose the fastening of the bag and insert themselves in its depths. Then with a little cry of joy, she drew out and held up, for all to view, the bronze box that had caused all the disturbance—the Dragon's Secret!

The complicated explanations were all over at last, and the curious, fragmentary story was pieced together. Detective Barnes took up the little bronze box and examined it carefully, experimenting, as they all had done, to find a way of opening it—and, of course, unsuccessfully.

"There's one thing that puzzles me, though," remarked Ted, "about that queer type-written note. How and why and by whom was it left originally?"

"It was written on thin, foreign-looking paper," replied the detective, "and I can only guess that the foreigners left it there, though probably not on their first trip that afternoon. No doubt they either went to the village, or, more likely, returned to the city to talk it over, perhaps with Gaines. And he, supposing I had long since captured the prize, and to put them off the scent, suggested that some one nearby may have been meddling with the matter and that they leave a warning for them. I feel rather certain he must have done this to gain time, for he knew that if I had found the thing, I would immediately set about having him released, and he must have wondered why I hadn't done so. Perhaps he thought I was having difficulty locating the house where they had him hidden. But, Great Scott!—that makes me think!—They must by this time have discovered the trick you played, Miss Phyllis, and be jumping mad over having been so fooled. Perhaps they think Gaines is responsible for it, and they'll certainly be making it hot for *him!* I must get to the city immediately and get him out of that hole. Oughtn't to waste another minute. If you can spare your car, Miss Eileen, I'd like to run up to the city with it, as I know there are no more trains to-night. I'll guarantee to fetch it and Gaines both back in the morning!"

"You certainly may have it," replied Eileen, "and you may take me with you and leave me at the hospital, on the way. Grandfather must know of this at once. I'm positive he'll recover now, since the worry is all over. But first, wouldn't you all like to see something? I happen to know the secret of opening this box. Grandfather showed it to me when I was a little girl, and he used to let me play with it."

She took a pin from her dress, inserted it into the carved eye of the dragon and pressed it in a certain fashion—and the lid of the bronze box flew up! They all pressed forward eagerly and gazed in. There lay the packet of foreign letters, safe and sound. Eileen lifted them and looked curiously underneath. Nothing else was in the box except some strange, thin bits of yellow, foreign paper covered with vague pictures and curious Chinese characters. They seemed to be so thin and old as to be almost falling to pieces.

"I don't know what *these* things are," she remarked, "but they probably have nothing to do with this affair, anyway. Grandfather was always picking up queer old things on his travels. But he must have thought them interesting, or he never would have kept them in here. But we must go now," she ended, closing the box. "And I'll see you dear people all to-morrow. This has surely been a wonderful night!"

But just as she was ready to go, she said: "Do show me the dusty shelf where this was hidden, please!" And then, as she stood gazing up at it, she exclaimed, "To think that it lay here behind those worn-out old kitchen things all the time we were so madly hunting for it! But perhaps it was the safest place, after all!"

The two girls escorted Eileen and Mr. Barnes to the door, Ted offering to see them to the car. As they came out on the porch, Leslie uttered a little cry of delight. The storm, which all had momentarily forgotten in the later excitement, was over. The ragged clouds were driving by in a strong northwest wind, and a few stars could be seen peeping through the rifts, while, best of all, the water had already retreated several feet, though the crash of the breakers was still tremendous.

As Leslie and Phyllis returned to the room, they were startled to see Aunt Marcia, in a dressing-gown, peering out of the door of her room and blinking sleepily.

"What on earth are you two girls doing up at this unearthly hour?" she inquired. "I woke and thought I heard voices and came out to see!"

"Oh, we've been talking and watching the storm!" laughed Leslie. "It's all over now, and the stars are shining. You'd better go back to bed, Aunt Marcia. The fire's out and it's very chilly!"

And as the good lady turned back into her room Leslie whispered to Phyllis, "And she slept through all *that*—and never knew! How can I be thankful enough!"

CHAPTER XIX
THE BIGGEST SURPRISE OF ALL

"PHYLLIS! I've got a nibble, Phyllis! I believe I can land him, too. And it will be the first I've really managed to catch!" Leslie began to play her line, her hands fairly trembling with excitement.

The two girls and Ted stood at the ocean's edge, almost directly in front of the bungalows, whiling away a glorious, crisp afternoon in striving to induce the reluctant fish to bite. For some reason or other, they seemed remarkably shy that day. Leslie's nibble had been the first suggestion of possible luck. Just as she was cautiously beginning to reel in her line a pair of hands was clasped over her eyes, and a gay voice laughed "Guess who!"

"Eileen!" cried Leslie, joyfully, forgetting all about her nibble. "Oh, but it's good to see you! We've missed you so since you left. Where *did* you come from?"

"Grandfather and I motored down to-day," replied Eileen, as they all crowded round her, "to stay over night at Aunt Sally's in the village. He's going to drive out here a little later, with Geoffrey at the wheel, because he wants to see you people. You know, we sail for England on Saturday, and he says he doesn't intend to leave before he has a chance to greet the friends who did so much for him! You've no idea how much better he is! He began to pick up the moment I told him the news that night; and in the two weeks since, he's been like another person. But he hates it in New York and it doesn't agree with him, and he just wanted to come down here once more before we left."

"But how did *you* get here, if he's coming later in the car?" demanded Phyllis.

"Oh, I *walked*, of course! It was a glorious day for it. Aunt Sally wondered so, to see me taking the air in anything but that car! What a dear she is! And how scandalously I had to treat her when I stayed there before. But the dear lady never suspected that I was in an agony of worry and suspense all the time, and didn't dare to be nice to her for fear I'd just be tempted to give way and tell the whole secret. I used to long to throw myself in her lap and boo-hoo on her shoulder! I've made it all up with her since, though! There's Grandfather now! Come up to the veranda, all of you, because he's not strong enough yet to walk on the sand."

They hurried up to the house and got there in time for Eileen to make the introductions. They were all deeply attracted to the tall, stooping, gray-haired, pleasant-mannered gentleman who greeted them so cordially—as if they were old and valued friends instead of such recent acquaintances.

"I'm going to ask you to let me sit awhile on your front veranda," he said. "I want to get a last impression of this lovely spot to carry away with me to England. Also, I would like to have a chat with you young folks and tell you how much I appreciate what you all did for us."

Rather embarrassed by his suggestion that there was anything to thank them for, Leslie led him through the house to the veranda facing the ocean. Here Aunt Marcia sat, wrapped to the eyes, enjoying the late October sunshine, the invigorating salt air, and the indescribable beauty of the changeful ocean. Leslie had long since, very cautiously and gradually, revealed to her the story of their adventure at Curlew's Nest. So carefully had she done so that any possible alarm Miss Marcia might have experienced was swallowed up in wonder at the marvelous way in which it had all turned out.

Leslie now introduced Mr. Ramsay, and they all gathered around him as he settled himself to enjoy the view. He chatted a while with Miss Marcia, compared notes with her on the effect of the climate on her health and his own, then turned to the young folks.

"It is quite useless for me," he began, "to try to express my appreciation of all you people have done for Eileen and myself in the little matter of the bronze box."

"But we must tell you," interrupted Phyllis, eagerly, "that we aren't going to sail under any false colors! We found that little box,—or rather, Rags here found it—and we didn't have a notion, of course, to whom it could belong and we were just wild to get it open and see what was in it. When we couldn't manage that, we hid it away in the safest place we could think of, to wait for what would happen. I'm afraid we didn't make any very desperate hunt for the owner, and when we suspected that Eileen might have something to do with it, I'm ashamed to say that we wouldn't give it up to her—at first—because we were annoyed at the way she acted. We didn't understand, of course, but that doesn't excuse it!"

"All that you say may be true," smiled Mr. Ramsay, "but that does not alter the fact that you delivered it up the moment you discovered the rightful owner. And Miss Phyllis's clever little ruse of burying the false box probably saved Geoffrey a bad time. For if those fellows hadn't found *something* there that night, they would certainly have made it hot for him. As it was, it gained us so much time that Detective

104 | P a g e

Barnes had a chance to get my man out of their clutches before they had done him any damage, though they were furious at being duped. They're all safely in jail now, and there is nothing more to fear from them. Of course, the principal who hired them is safe, over in China, but he didn't gain *his* point,—and that's the main thing! As for the letters, I concluded that, after all, my ideas as to how to keep them safely were out of date, and they have long since been forwarded to Washington, in care of Barnes, and are now in the hands of my country's representative there. I shall not concern myself any further about their security."

He put his hands in his pocket and drew out the little bronze casket. Then he went on,—

"This little box has had some strange adventures in its day, but nothing stranger than the one it has just passed through. It has, however, something else in it, that I thought might be of interest to you, and so I have brought it along and will explain about it." He opened the box in the same way as Eileen had done and revealed to their curious gaze the fragile old bits of paper they had seen on that eventful night. He took them out, fingered them thoughtfully, and handed one to each of the four young folks.

"There is a strange little adventure connected with these that perhaps you may be interested to hear," he continued. "It happened when I was passing through the city of Peking, some years ago, during their revolution. There was a good deal of lawlessness rife at the time, and bands of natives were running about, pillaging and looting anything they thought it safe to tamper with. One day, in one of the open places of the city, I happened along just in time to see ten or a dozen lawless natives pulling from its pedestal a great bronze idol, hideous as they make 'em, that had stood there probably for uncounted centuries. When they got it to the ground, they found it to be hollow inside, as most of the really ancient ones are, and filled with all manner of articles representing the sacrifices that had been made to it, through the ages, and placed inside it by their priests. These articles included everything from real jewels of undoubted value to papier-mâché imitations of food—a device the Chinese often use in sacrificing to the idols.

"Of course, the mob made an immediate grab for the jewels, but it had begun to make my blood boil to see them making off with so much unlawful booty. So, almost without thinking, I snatched out my revolver, placed myself in front of the pile, and shouted to them that I would shoot the first one who laid a finger on the stuff. And in the same breath I sent Geoffrey hurrying to find some of the city authorities to come and rescue what would probably be some thousands of dollars' worth of gems.

"Fortunately, I was armed with an effective weapon and they were not. So I managed to hold the fort till Geoffrey returned with the authorities, and on seeing them, the mob promptly melted away. The mandarin wanted to present me with some of the jewels, in gratitude for my services, but I had no wish for them and only asked permission to take with me a few of these little scraps of paper, which had been among the medley of articles in the idol's interior. Of course they assented, deeming me, no doubt, a very stupid 'foreign devil' to be so easily satisfied! I have carried them about with me for several years, and now I am going to give them to you young folks—one to each of you, as a little token of my gratitude for your invaluable help!"

He sat back in his chair, smiling benignly, while he watched the bewilderment on all their faces. Ted, Phyllis, and Leslie were striving to hide this, under a polite assumption of intense gratitude, though they were a bit puzzled as to why he should choose *them*, of all people, who had no very great interest in such things, as recipients of this special gift. But his own granddaughter was under less compulsion to assume what she did not feel.

"This is awfully good of you, Granddaddy!" she cried, "but I don't honestly see what the big idea is! I think that story of yours was ripping, but I don't exactly know what to do with this little bit of paper. It seems so old and frail, too, that I'm almost afraid a breath will blow it to pieces. I really think it will be safer in your care."

He was still smiling indulgently. "I suspected that the outspoken Eileen would voice the general opinion of this gift! I don't mind it in the least, and I don't blame you a bit for feeling a trifle bewildered about the matter. But I haven't told you the whole story yet. To continue! As I said before, I carried these bits of paper around with me for a number of years, simply because they reminded me of my little adventure. Then, one day early this past summer, on the steamer coming across the Pacific, I chanced to meet a man connected with the British Museum whom I soon discovered to be one of the principal experts on Chinese antiquities. And it occurred to me to show him these bits of paper and ask if he could imagine what they were. He examined them carefully and then came to me in great delight, declaring that they certainly were, beyond a shadow of doubt, the oldest existing specimens of Chinese *paper money!*

"And he added, moreover, that the British Museum had no specimens in its possession as old as these, and declared that he believed the Museum would be delighted to buy them, probably for three or four hundred pounds apiece!"

The listening four gasped and stared at him incredulously, but he went on undisturbed. "I said I would think the matter over and decide when I reached

England. But meantime, for reasons which I have already enlarged upon, I have decided instead to give them to you, as a little testimonial of my deep gratitude. If, by any chance, *you* should decide that you would prefer to have the money, I will attempt to negotiate the sale for you when I reach London and—"

He got no further for, with a whoop of joy, Ted sprang forward and laid his bit in Mr. Ramsay's lap and the others followed his example, striving very inadequately to express their wonder and delight.

But he interrupted them, smilingly. "I should like to inquire, just as a matter of curiosity, what form of investment each one of you expects to make with the sum you receive? Don't think me too inquisitive please. It's just an old man's curiosity!"

"I've decided already!" cried Eileen. "I'm going to spend mine on another trip over here in the spring to visit you girls, and I'm going to bring mother with me. I wouldn't have got here this time if it hadn't been for Grandfather, for Daddy simply put his foot down and said he couldn't afford it. And next year Grandfather may be in Timbuctoo or somewhere like it, and I wouldn't have a chance. But I've just *got* to see you all again soon, for you're the best friends I ever made."

"And I'm going to save mine for some extra expensive courses in chemical engineering in college that I never supposed I could afford to take," declared Ted. "I expected I'd have to go into business after I graduated, for a year or two, till I scraped up enough, but now I can go right on."

"Of course, I'll get my music now," cried Phyllis, "and I'm the happiest girl alive!"

"Well, it's hardly necessary for me to say that now little Ralph will have his chance to be strong and well, like other boys," murmured Leslie, tears of joy standing in her eyes.

Then, to ease the tension of the almost too happy strain, Mr. Ramsay continued:

"But there is another member of this party that it would not do to forget!" He drew from his pocket a handsome leather and silver dog-collar, called Rags over to him, and, as the dog ambled up, gravely addressed him:

"Kindly accept this token of my immense gratitude and allow me to clasp it about your neck!" Rags submitted gravely while his old collar was removed and the new one put in place, and immediately after began to make frantic efforts to get it off over his head! ButMr. Ramsay only laughed and held up a five dollar bill, adding:

"I realize that you do not entirely appreciate this gift at present. In fact, I sympathize with you in thinking it a decided nuisance! But here is something else that may soothe your sorrow—a five-dollar bill, to be devoted exclusively to the purchase of luscious steaks, tender chops, and juicy bones—for your solitary delectation!"

Amid the general laughter that followed, he added: "And now, may I ask that you escort me over to the veranda of Curlew's Nest? I have a great desire to walk up and down on that porch for a few moments and think of all the strange adventures of which that delightful little bungalow has been the scene!"

And accompanied by Rags, still striving madly to scrape off his new collar by rubbing it in the sand, they escorted their guest to Curlew's Nest!

End of the book.